In/Famous People

HISTORY BITES

Volume 2

Solomon Schmidt

Copyright © 2019 by Solomon Schmidt

All rights reserved. No part of this book may be reproduced or transmitted in any form or by any means, electronic or mechanical, including photocopying and recording, or by any information storage and retrieval system, without permission in writing by the author.

This book is dedicated to my parents, who have taught me about life, encouraged me in my faith, and supported my passion for history. I love them very much.

And to Walter Hooper, who was C.S. Lewis's secretary in 1963, a friend of J.R.R. Tolkien for ten years, and an admired acquaintance of Pope John Paul II. His friendly correspondences with me have been a source of encouragement and help throughout my time of study of famous people from world history.

A Note From the Author

    In/Famous People History Bites Volume 2 is an overview of fifty of some of the most in/famous people from world history, covering from Mark Twain to Tiger Woods. I selected world leaders, authors, religious figures, scientists, and athletes who I believed were some of the most in/famous and influential people in each category. My goal was to select historical figures with whom most people are familiar.

    This book serves as a great read-aloud but can also be enjoyed by independent readers of all ages. I really hope you enjoy it.

~Solomon

TABLE OF CONTENTS

#		Pages
1.	Mark Twain	1–4
2.	Thomas Edison	5–8
3.	Alexander Graham Bell	9–12
4.	Vincent van Gogh	13–16
5.	Sigmund Freud	17–20
6.	Woodrow Wilson	21–24
7.	Theodore Roosevelt	25–28
8.	Henry Ford	29–32
9.	Wright Brothers	33–36
10.	Mohandas Gandhi	37–40
11.	Vladimir Lenin	41–44
12.	Winston Churchill	45–48
13.	Josef Stalin	49–52
14.	Albert Einstein	53–56
15.	Pablo Picasso	57–60
16.	Franklin D. Roosevelt	61–64
17.	Harry Truman	65–68
18.	Adolf Hitler	69–72
19.	Agatha Christie	73–76
20.	Dwight D. Eisenhower	77–80
21.	J.R.R. Tolkien	81–84
22.	Mao Zedong	85–88
23.	Babe Ruth	89–92
24.	Amelia Earhart	93–96
25.	C.S. Lewis	97–100

26.	Walt Disney	101–104
27.	George Orwell	105–108
28.	Mother Teresa	109–112
29.	Ronald Reagan	113–116
30.	Lucille Ball	117–120
31.	Jesse Owens	121–124
32.	John F. Kennedy	125–128
33.	Nelson Mandela	129–132
34.	Pope John Paul II	133–136
35.	Fidel Castro	137–140
36.	Martin Luther King Jr.	141–144
37.	Mikhail Gorbachev	145–148
38.	Elvis Presley	149–152
39.	John Lennon	153–156
40.	Muhammad Ali	157–160
41.	Donald J. Trump	161–164
42.	George W. Bush	165–168
43.	Steve Jobs	169–172
44.	Bill Gates	173–176
45.	Michael Jackson	177–180
46.	Princess Diana	181–184
47.	Barack Obama	185–188
48.	Michael Jordan	189–192
49.	J.K. Rowling	193–196
50.	Tiger Woods	197–200

Mark Twain
1835 – 1910

Mark Twain

Born: November 30, 1835, in Florida, Missouri

Died: April 21, 1910, at his country home, Stormfield, in Redding, Connecticut

Wife: Olivia Langdon (married 1870-1904)

Children: Langdon, Susy, Clara, Jean

Samuel Langhorne Clemens grew up on the banks of the Mississippi River in Missouri and was fascinated by the business and dangers of life along the river. He spent much of his early life traveling as a printer in cities like New York City and Philadelphia. He later became a steamboat river pilot until the start of the American Civil War (1861-1865). The experiences on the Mississippi River gave Samuel Clemens inspiration later on in life when he wrote *The Adventures of Tom Sawyer* and *The Adventures of Huckleberry Finn*.

In 1863, Mr. Clemens gave himself the pen name of "Mark Twain" while writing for the *Territorial Enterprise* newspaper of Virginia City, Nevada. In 1865, he published a short story called "The Celebrated Jumping Frog of Calaveras County," which became very popular around the country. In 1869, he published a book called *The Innocents Abroad*, which was based on his travels to Europe, Egypt, and Israel. Mr. Twain continued to write and travel, and from mid-1873 to early 1874, he gave a few different lectures around England in cities like London and Leicester. One of these lectures was called "Sandwich Islands," and in it, he described the Sandwich Islands (present-day Hawaii) based on memories of his visit there in 1866.

In 1876, Mr. Twain published *The Adventures of Tom Sawyer*, which was a story about a young boy named Tom Sawyer, who lived along the banks of the Mississippi River in the fictional town of St. Petersburg. It was well-received and became very popular. In 1881, he published *The Prince and the Pauper*, and in 1884, *The Adventures of Huckleberry Finn* (the sequel to *Tom Sawyer*) was published.

The Adventures of Tom Sawyer and *The Adventures of Huckleberry Finn* have sold millions of copies around the world and are considered by many people to be some of the greatest books of American literature.

Mark Twain was also very popular for his funny short stories. Some of his most famous ones include "Advice to Little Girls" (1867), "The Private History of a Campaign That Failed" (1885), and "Hunting the Deceitful Turkey" (1906). Many of his humorous stories were published after his death in a large book called *The Comic Mark Twain Reader* (1977).

Many films and TV shows have been made based on Mr. Twain's books. He was one of the most famous and popular American authors in history, and his stories are still beloved by many people today.

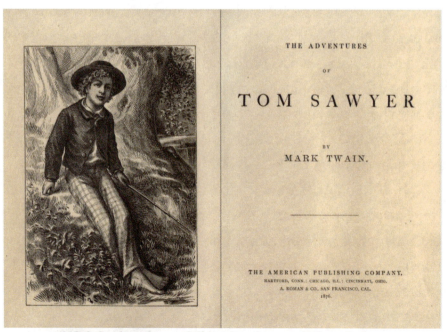

1876 first edition of The Adventures of Tom Sawyer

Map of the Mississippi River

Mark Twain at his writing desk

FUN FACT

Mark Twain's fictional character Huckleberry Finn is based on a boy named Tom Blankenship, whom Mr. Twain knew while growing up in Hannibal, Missouri.

Thomas Edison
1847 – 1931

Thomas Edison

Born: February 11, 1847, in Milan, Ohio

Died: October 18, 1931, at his home, "Glenmont," in West Orange, New Jersey

Wives: Mary Stilwell (married 1871–1884), Mina Miller (married 1886–1931)

Children: Marion, Thomas, Jr., William, Madeleine, Charles, Theodore

Thomas Edison did not do well in school and was only formally educated outside of the home for a few months. Eventually, he was taken out of school and was homeschooled by his mother, Nancy. Thomas worked at a number of different jobs as a young man, including selling candy and newspapers on board a train. One time, while working at this job, when he was just fourteen years old, Thomas saved a young boy from being hit by a moving train. The young boy's father was so thankful to Thomas for saving his son's life that he offered to train him as a telegraph officer. The telegraph was an old-fashioned way of communicating messages along a wire.

A few years later, Thomas went to work for a telegraph company called Western Union in Kentucky. He was fascinated by communication and also had a great interest in science, especially chemistry. He spent several years working on different inventions, and in 1869, he received his first patent (the right to an invention) for his electrographic vote recorder. This machine was designed for the United States Congress to use in casting votes with electrical switches. That same year, he also developed an improved version of the stock ticker, which was first invented in 1867 by Edward Callahan for telegraph wires.

Mr. Edison continued experimenting and inventing, and in 1876, he moved to Menlo Park, New Jersey, where he established a large research laboratory. In 1878, he received a patent for his invention called the phonograph, a sound-recording machine that made Mr. Edison famous. In 1880, he received a patent for his incandescent lightbulb. This was not the first lightbulb invented, but a greatly improved one.

Mr. Edison continued to develop and invent many things, including DC (Direct Current) Electricity in 1882. He also invented two important machines with William Dickson: the Kinetograph, which was a motion picture (movie) camera, and the Kinetoscope, which was a viewer that people looked through to watch motion pictures/movies.

By the end of his life, Mr. Edison had received over 1,000 patents for his own inventions as well as for many improvements made to other people's inventions. He also founded many companies, including the Edison Illuminating Company (early 1880s) and General Electric (1892), which is still a very successful company today.

Thomas Edison was one of the most famous and influential inventors of all time, and some of his inventions are still used all around the world today.

Thomas Edison with his phonograph

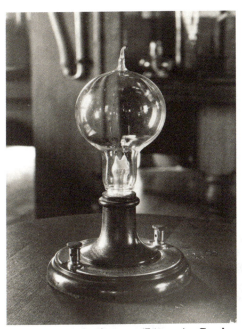

Replica of Thomas Edison's first incandescent lightbulb

Thomas Edison with his Kinetoscope

FUN FACT

The first words that Thomas Edison recorded on the phonograph were the opening lines of a famous nursery rhyme: "Mary had a little lamb; its fleece was white as snow. And everywhere that Mary went, the lamb was sure to go."

Alexander Graham Bell
1847 – 1922

Alexander Graham Bell

Born: March 3, 1847, in Edinburgh, Scotland

Died: August 2, 1922, at his estate, Beinn Bhreagh, on Cape Breton Island, Nova Scotia, Canada

Wife: Mabel Hubbard (married 1877-1922)

Children: Elsie, Marian, Edward, Robert

Alexander Graham Bell enjoyed inventing things and learning about the science of sound from the time he was very young. At just twelve years old, he created his first invention, which was a dehusking machine for a grain mill.

Interestingly, Alexander's mother, Eliza, and his wife, Mabel, were both deaf. Throughout his life, Alexander did a lot to help deaf people, including creating a method of teaching them how to speak called oralism. This involves lip reading and imitating mouth shapes and breathing patterns of speech. He actually met and examined Helen Keller when she was just six years old. After getting seriously ill as a baby, Helen became deaf and blind. Mr. Bell was able to help her learn how to communicate, and he also helped her parents find her teacher, Anne Sullivan.

In 1872, he started a school in Boston for teachers of the deaf. In 1873, Mr. Bell became Professor of Vocal Physiology and Elocution (science of the human voice) at the Boston University School of Oratory. He continued to experiment with sound and wanted to find a way to send voice signals across a telegraph wire, which were used during that time to send Morse code signals. Morse code is a communication system in which messages are sent across a telegraph wire and words are written down using signals called dots and dashes.

After many experiments and working with a mechanic named Thomas Watson, Mr. Bell most famously and successfully invented the telephone. On March 10, 1876, he made the first telephone call in history. He was speaking to Mr. Watson and said, "Mr. Watson, come here. I want to see you." Mr. Bell quickly got a patent for his invention because other people were experimenting with the idea at the time, and he wanted to be the first person to have the rights to the invention. In 1876, he showcased (presented) his invention at the Centennial Exhibition in Philadelphia, Pennsylvania, and continued to demonstrate it at other places.

In 1877, the Bell Telephone Company was founded, and it is called AT&T today. Mr. Bell's invention began to sell very well all across the United States. In 1890, he founded the American Association to Promote the Teaching of Speech to the Deaf. In 1915, Mr. Bell made the first successful transcontinental telephone call all the way from New York City, New York, to San Francisco, California.

Alexander Graham Bell invented several other important things in his life, including the metal detector and a sonar device to locate icebergs under water. He was one of the most famous and influential inventors of all time.

Replica of the 1876 telephone, invented by Alexander Graham Bell

Mr. Bell using his telephone to call from New York City to Chicago, Illinois, in 1892

Helen Keller and Alexander Graham Bell

FUN FACT

Between 1898-1903, Mr. Bell served as the second president of the National Geographic Society. During this time, he was influential in printing more pictures and photographs in the *National Geographic* magazine than any other previous president of the Society.

Vincent van Gogh
1853 - 1890

Vincent van Gogh

Born: March 30, 1853, in Zundert, Netherlands

Died: July 29, 1890, in Auvers-sur-Oise, France

Wife: None

Children: None

Vincent van Gogh's father, Theodorus, was a minister, and three of his uncles were art dealers. From an early age, Vincent liked to draw, but he worked at several different jobs before he became a full-time artist. He worked at art dealerships in The Hague, Netherlands, and London, England, and was also a minister in Borinage, Belgium. However, he never actually received a college education in theology (the study of God), and in 1879, he decided that he was not cut out to be a minister. So, one year later, in 1880, Mr. van Gogh moved to Brussels, Belgium, and became an artist.

Mr. van Gogh's first drawings were done with pencils, charcoal sticks, and/or watercolors. His most famous painting from his early period as an artist is called *The Potato Eaters* (1885). In 1886, Mr. van Gogh moved to Paris, France, to learn a new style of painting called Impressionism. This style focuses on small, thin brush strokes and the correct representation of light. During this time, he painted over twenty self-portraits. In 1888, Mr. van Gogh moved to Arles, France, where he continued to paint and was inspired by the energy and bright sunshine of the city.

Unfortunately, Mr. van Gogh was not totally right in his mind at certain times throughout his life, and in late 1888, he threatened his friend Paul Gauguin (who was also an artist) with a razor. After Mr. Gauguin escaped, Mr. van Gogh used the razor blade to cut off part of his own left ear. In 1889, he went to live in a hospital for mentally ill people, called the Saint-Paul-de-Mausole asylum in Saint-Rémy-de-Provence, France. During this difficult time, he painted his most famous work, called *Starry Night* (1889), which is one of the most famous paintings of all time.

Sadly, in 1890, while painting one day in the summer, Mr. van Gogh killed himself. Since his death, Vincent van Gogh has become one of the most famous artists of all time. He completed over 800 oil paintings and over 1,300 watercolor paintings, drawings, and sketches. Some of his paintings have been sold for tens of millions of dollars. Two of his most famous paintings are *Café Terrace at Night* (1888) and *Irises* (1889).

Starry Night by Vincent van Gogh

Café Terrace at Night *by* Vincent van Gogh

FUN FACT

During the time he lived in Paris, France, Vincent van Gogh became interested in Japanese art. He especially liked Japanese woodcuts, which are made by carving a picture into a block of wood. Mr. van Gogh bought 660 Japanese woodcuts from an art dealer in Paris.

Sigmund Freud
1856 - 1939

Sigmund Freud

Born: May 6, 1856, in Freiberg (present-day Příbor) in present-day Czech Republic (which was part of the Austrian Empire at that time)

Died: September 23, 1939, in London, England

Wife: Martha Bernays (married 1886-1939)

Children: Mathilde, Martin, Oliver, Ernst, Sophie, Anna

Sigmund Freud's father, Jakob, and his mother, Amalia, were both Jews, and they raised Sigmund in the Jewish faith. He grew up reading The Torah, which is the Jewish Scripture and contains the first five books of the Old Testament of the Bible (also called the Pentateuch). When he was older, from 1873-1881, Sigmund studied medicine at the University of Vienna in Vienna, Austria, where he lived and worked most of his life. He was especially interested in neurology, which is the study of the human brain and nervous system.

From 1882-1886, Mr. Freud worked at the Vienna General Hospital and continued his study of the brain. In 1885, he studied in Paris, France, under Jean-Martin Charcot, who influenced Mr. Freud's idea of psychoanalysis. Mr. Freud also studied the ideas of Charles Darwin and Friedrich Nietzsche, both of whom were atheists. He eventually abandoned his childhood Jewish faith, became an atheist, and was strongly opposed to any ideas about God.

In 1886, Mr. Freud set up his own psychiatric practice in Vienna, Austria, where he would examine patients who needed psychological (mental) help. He began to develop influential ideas about psychoanalysis, which is a method of trying to treat mental illness by deeply searching a person's conscious and unconscious thoughts. Conscious thought is thinking that can be controlled, while unconscious thought cannot be directly controlled. Psychoanalysis teaches that humans are not responsible for their wrongdoings. Mr. Freud also taught that happiness was the chief purpose of a person's life and that religion and religious beliefs were a type of sickness. He believed that the human personality was made up of three elements: the id, ego, and superego. He taught that people's belief in God was just an illusion (wrong understanding), and he once said, "Religion is the universal obsessional neurosis of the people."

Mr. Freud talked about his idea of psychoanalysis and religion in many books, including *Studies in Hysteria* (1895), *The Interpretation of Dreams* (1900), *The Future of an Illusion* (1927), *Civilization and Its Discontents* (1930), and *Moses and Monotheism* (1939). His ideas eventually became famous around the world, and he gathered followers, who also became psychoanalysts. People who believe in and/or practice his form of psychology are known as Freudian.

In 1938, because he was a Jew, Mr. Freud left Austria to escape the German Nazis, who hated and killed many Jews. He went to London, England, where he lived for the last year of his life. Sadly, he asked a doctor to end his life by giving him an overdose of drugs, and he died.

Sigmund Freud's ideas have had a huge impact on the way people think about themselves and others. He was one of the most in/famous and influential philosophers of all time.

The sofa in Sigmund Freud's office in which clients would lie down and he would psychoanalyze them

Sigmund Freud at his writing desk

INTERESTING FACT

In 1925, movie producer Samuel Goldwyn, of Metro-Goldwyn-Mayer (MGM) movie studios, asked Mr. Freud to write a script for a movie about some of the greatest love stories in world history. He offered Mr. Freud $100,000 as payment for the job, but Mr. Freud turned down the offer.

Woodrow Wilson
1856 - 1924

Woodrow Wilson

Born: December 28, 1856, in Staunton, Virginia

Died: February 3, 1924, in Washington, D.C., United States

Wives: Ellen Axson (married 1885-1914), Edith Bolling (married 1915-1924)

Children: Margaret, Jessie, Eleanor

Thomas Woodrow Wilson grew up in Augusta, Georgia, and his father was the pastor of First Presbyterian Church there. His childhood home was used as a hospital for soldiers during the Civil War, and this greatly influenced Thomas's opinions about war. Eventually, Thomas became known by his middle name Woodrow.

In 1875, Woodrow enrolled at Princeton University in New Jersey. While there, he participated in sports and also in writing and speaking groups. In 1879, Woodrow graduated from Princeton and went on to Johns Hopkins University. In 1886, he graduated from Johns Hopkins University, earning a doctorate (PhD) degree in political science. After earning his PhD, Mr. Wilson became the president of Princeton University, and this helped him to gain popularity throughout the state of New Jersey.

In 1910, Mr. Wilson began his political career when he was elected the governor of New Jersey, and he served in that position for two years. In 1912, the Republican Party of the United States was divided. Some of the Republicans supported Theodore Roosevelt while others supported President William Howard Taft. The Democratic Party saw this as an opportunity to win the next election, so they decided to nominate Woodrow Wilson as their presidential candidate. In 1912, he won the election in a landslide and became America's twenty-eighth president.

While he was president, Mr. Wilson began a new banking and business system, called the Federal Reserve System. This meant the banking and business systems in America were now controlled by the federal government, and it gave the U.S. government a lot of power. Woodrow Wilson is known for his support of increased government control over public policies.

In 1914, World War I began and involved many countries around the world. Germany and Austria-Hungary and their allies (called the Central Powers) were fighting against England, France, Russia, and other countries (called the Allies). President Wilson decided to not get America involved, and many Americans appreciated how he kept them out of the war. Because of this, he remained popular and was reelected as president in 1916. However, only a few months after his reelection, President Wilson decided to enter America into the war because the Germans had sunk an American merchant ship called the *William P. Frye*.

During World War I, President Wilson signed laws (like the Alien Friends Act) that forced people to leave America if they had opinions against the war. This is called deportation. Government workers were also sent to spy on Americans who opposed the war to make sure that they were speaking well of and remaining loyal to America (the Sedition Act of 1918).

In 1918, the Allies won World War I, and President Wilson traveled to Paris, France, to discuss peace negotiations with Germany. While there, he presented his idea of the League of Nations to help establish peace between countries. Because of this idea, in 1920, President Wilson received the Nobel Peace Prize. That same year, the 19th Amendment to the U.S. Constitution was also adopted, and it gave women the right to vote in America.

Woodrow Wilson was one of the most popular U.S. presidents and world leaders in history.

"Big Four" Leaders at the Paris Peace Conference, after the end of WWI; From left to right: David Lloyd George (British Prime Minister), Vittorio Emanuele Orlando (Italian Prime Minister), Georges Clemenceau (French Prime Minister), and President Woodrow Wilson

FUN FACT

Woodrow Wilson's face was on the 100,000 dollar bill, but it is no longer used today.

Theodore Roosevelt
1858 - 1919

Theodore Roosevelt

Born: October 27, 1858, in New York City, New York

Died: January 6, 1919, at his home, the "Summer White House," in Oyster Bay, New York

Wives: Alice Lee (married 1880-1884), Edith Carow (married 1886-1919)

Children: Alice, Theodore Jr., Kermit, Ethel, Archibald, Quentin

While growing up, Theodore Roosevelt had many health problems. He was sick most of the time and suffered from stomach aches, painful headaches, and asthma. Theodore tried many things to get better, but most of the remedies did not help. His father, Theodore Sr., told him to exercise more, so Theodore obeyed his father, and his health began to improve. He especially enjoyed swimming, hiking, and boxing and really loved being outdoors. In addition to sports, Theodore also loved reading about American history.

After finishing school, Theodore attended Harvard University, and in 1880, he graduated from college. He thought about becoming a lawyer but decided to go into politics instead. In 1882, Mr. Roosevelt was elected as a New York State assemblyman. While in New York, he also worked as a policeman and was elected as one of four police commissioners of New York City.

In 1897, Mr. Roosevelt went to work as Assistant Secretary of the U.S. Navy under President William McKinley. When the Spanish-American War began in 1898, Mr. Roosevelt gathered a fighting group together called "The Rough Riders." They fought in Cuba and won an important battle on San Juan Hill. This made Mr. Roosevelt very famous and led to him becoming William McKinley's vice presidential candidate during President McKinley's second term.

Sadly, President McKinley was shot and killed in 1901 during his second term, and Mr. Roosevelt immediately became America's next president. During his presidency, Mr. Roosevelt tried to stop big businesses from taking over smaller businesses. He was also opposed to the government controlling businesses and wanted capitalism to grow.

Capitalism is an economic system that encourages private ownership of businesses and personal income and profit.

President Roosevelt made many foreign policy agreements and one of them included overseeing the construction of the Panama Canal. This is a waterway that connects the Atlantic Ocean and the Pacific Ocean across Latin America. This was important because it allowed boats to travel more quickly to different places of the world, helping to increase trade between countries.

President Roosevelt also helped to create many of America's National Parks under the Forest Reserve Act, including Yosemite National Park. Because of this, forests, mountains, and animals were protected and preserved for recreational use.

After his two presidential terms ended in 1909, President Roosevelt took a trip to Europe. After he returned to America, he ran for president again in 1912 against Woodrow Wilson and William Howard Taft but lost.

Theodore Roosevelt was one of the most popular American presidents and is one of only four presidents whose face is carved on Mt. Rushmore in South Dakota.

President William McKinley and Theodore Roosevelt

Mt. Rushmore in South Dakota

FUN FACT

Theodore Roosevelt created many expressions, including "good to the last drop," which became the Maxwell House Coffee slogan. President Roosevelt was known to drink up to a gallon of coffee every day.

Henry Ford
1863 – 1947

Henry Ford

Born: July 30, 1863, in Greenfield Township, Michigan

Died: April 7, 1947, at his estate, Fair Lane, in Dearborn, Michigan

Wife: Clara Jane Bryant (married 1888-1947)

Children: Edsel

In 1876, when Henry Ford was only twelve years old, his mother, Mary, died. His father, William, wanted him to take over the family farm in Greenfield Township, Michigan, but Henry did not have any interest in farming. At the age of sixteen, he left home and got a job in Detroit, Michigan, as an apprentice machinist for a shipbuilding company. An apprentice machinist is someone who learns a lot about machines from an expert craftsman.

In 1891, the Edison Illuminating Company (as in Thomas Edison, the famous inventor) hired Henry as an engineer. While working at this job, Henry started to experiment with engines and horseless carriages, which is an old-fashioned term for cars. He also became good friends with Mr. Edison himself.

In 1896, Mr. Ford developed his first model for a car, called the Ford Quadricycle. Mr. Edison encouraged Mr. Ford in his efforts, which led to Mr. Ford making more models of cars. In 1899, Mr. Ford left the Edison Illuminating Company, and in 1903, he founded the Ford Motor Company. In 1908, he introduced the revolutionary (new and extraordinary) Model T, which had much better functions than most cars at that time, including the fact that it was easier to drive and repair. The Model T eventually became the best-selling car in America. This was mainly because, beginning in 1913, Mr. Ford used assembly-line production very effectively. Although Mr. Ford did not invent the car or the assembly line, he was able to manufacture and sell his Model T's to Americans at a much cheaper price than other cars.

In addition to his machinery skills and inventions, Mr. Ford was also very interested in politics and war. During World War I (1914-1918), Mr. Ford was against the war and desired peace between the nations that were involved. This is called pacifism. He was also known for promoting controversial content through his newspaper *The Dearborn Independent* and the book *The International Jew*. Mr. Ford was an anti-Semite, which means that he did not like Jewish people, and his opinions had an influence on Adolf Hitler and the development of Nazism. In 1938, he was actually given an award by Adolf Hitler for his anti-Semitic writings.

Despite these facts, Henry Ford was one of the most famous and influential industrialists and inventors of all time. The Ford Motor Company is still one of the most successful car companies in the world today.

Henry Ford on his 1896 Quadricycle

Henry Ford (left) and Thomas Edison (right)

1908 Model T

FUN FACT

In 1918, Henry Ford ran for a seat in the United States Senate as a Democrat from Michigan. However, he lost to Republican Truman Newberry and never ran for political office again after that.

Wright Brothers
1867 – 1912 / 1871 – 1948

Wright Brothers:
Orville (left) and Wilbur (right)

Born: Wilbur: April 16, 1867, in Millville, Indiana
Orville: August 19, 1871, in Dayton, Ohio

Died: Wilbur: May 30, 1912, in Dayton, Ohio
Orville: January 30, 1948, in Dayton, Ohio

Wives: Neither married

Children: Neither had children

While growing up in Ohio, the Wright Brothers (Wilbur and Orville) loved to invent and create things. In 1878, their father, Milton, gave them a toy helicopter that sparked their interest in flying, and they began to experiment with their own helicopters. Orville also liked to build and construct kites. As they got a little older, the brothers experimented with different flying principles using kites and eventually gliders, which are lightweight aircraft that do not have engines.

In 1889, the brothers began to run their own printing business in Dayton, Ohio, and they published a few small newspapers, pamphlets, and other things. They later sold this business in 1899. In 1892, they opened up their own bicycle shop in Dayton, called the Wright Cycle Exchange (later called the Wright Cycle Company). While in this business, the brothers became better designers and engineers and continued experimenting with the possibility of flight. At this time in history, there were no airplanes and no one had ever flown in an engine-powered machine before.

The Wright Brothers worked on building a lightweight, but powerful aeroplane (old-fashioned term for an airplane) engine and designing ways to control the aircraft so that it would be stable. They also designed propellers that would work well and not be easily broken.

Around the beginning of the 1900s, the Wright Brothers went to Kitty Hawk, North Carolina, which is a very breezy, sandy area and was a good place to test their aeroplane model. On December 17, 1903, the first flight in history took place when Orville flew their model, called the

Wright Flyer, for twelve seconds, traveling 120 feet. At first, some people who were also trying to be the first in flight did not believe that the brothers had actually flown. However, even though people were critical of them, Wilbur and Orville continued to design better models of aeroplanes than their first one.

In 1906, they received a patent (right to an invention) for their aeroplane's three-axis control system. In 1908, Orville made the first flight that was over one-hour long at Fort Myer, Virginia. That same year, Wilbur made over 100 flights in France that many people witnessed (saw). The brothers continued to promote and improve their invention until Wilbur died in 1912.

The Wright Brothers were two of the most famous and influential designers and inventors of all time, and their invention of the airplane forever changed the world.

Wright Brothers' bicycle shop in Dayton, Ohio

Photo of the first flight: December 17, 1903, in Kitty Hawk, North Carolina (Orville is the one flying)

FUN FACT

Another famous person in aviation history was Neil Armstrong, who, in 1969, became the first person to walk on the moon. He carried a piece of fabric from the left wing of the 1903 Wright Flyer as well as a piece of wood from its propeller with him when he walked on the moon.

Mahatma Gandhi
1869 - 1948

Mahatma Gandhi

Born: October 2, 1869, in Porbandar, Gujarat, India

Died: January 30, 1948, in New Delhi, India

Wife: Kasturba Kapadia (married 1882-1948)

Children: His first son died just a few days after he was born, and his name is unknown. He and his wife also had Harilal, Manilal, Ramdas, and Devdas.

At the age of nineteen, Mohandas Karamchand Gandhi went to England to study law at University College London, which is a public research university. During this time, he became interested in Hindu texts and the teachings of Jesus Christ in the Bible. Hinduism is a religion that is practiced mostly in South Asia.

A few years later, Mohandas returned to his home country, India, and practiced law there. However, his law practice was not very successful, so he moved to South Africa, where he worked at another law office. It was here in South Africa that Mr. Gandhi began fighting for civil rights when he opposed apartheid, a policy of segregation against non-whites in South Africa. In 1915, Mr. Gandhi returned to India and began his work for the home rule movement, which was a group of people who wanted India to become its own independent country, separate from the British Empire.

Mr. Gandhi led non-violent campaigns in India during which many Indian people peacefully protested against the British government by striking (refusing to work), fasting (refusing to eat for a certain amount of time), and other things. Mr. Gandhi based his peaceful resistance on *satyagraha*, which is a term that he created and means "truth force" in Hindi. He also fought for the rights of poor people in India called the "untouchables."

At times, the British government responded to Gandhi's peaceful protests with violence, and they killed many Indian people. Mr. Gandhi was even arrested several times. In 1930, Mr. Gandhi led his most successful protest, called the Salt March, and it was against the British tax on salt. He led thousands of Indian people to the Arabian Sea in Dand, a village in India, in order to gather salt from the sea so they would not have to pay taxes to the British for it.

After World War II ended in 1945, Great Britain agreed to give India its independence. However, the Muslims in India wanted to separate India into two countries so that they could be separate from the Hindus. To avoid more violence, the British government agreed to the separation of the two groups. The Islamic Republic (Islam is the religion of Muslims) of Pakistan was established on August 14, 1947. The next day, the Republic of India was established. Today, they are simply called Pakistan and India, respectively.

Mr. Gandhi had hoped that the Hindus and Muslims could live together peacefully, but this did not happen. Sadly, on January 30, 1948, Mr. Ghandi was assassinated by an angry Hindu terrorist named Nathuram Godse, who did not like that Gandhi was peaceable to the Muslims and the "untouchables."

Mohandas Gandhi was one of the most famous and influential civil rights leaders of all time. He is more commonly known as Mahatma Gandhi. "Mahatma" means "great soul" in Hindi and is similar to the title of "Saint" in the Roman Catholic Church.

Mahatma Gandhi leading the Salt March in 1930

The Rajiv Gandhi Sea Link in the Bay of Mahim near Mumbai, India
(It is named after Mahatma Gandhi and is the longest bridge in India)

FUN FACT

In 1982, a movie called *Gandhi*, directed by Richard Attenborough, was released, and it was based on Mahatma Gandhi's life. It won an Academy Award for Best Picture.

Vladimir Lenin
1870 - 1924

Vladimir Lenin

Born: April 22, 1870, in Simbirsk (present-day Ulyanovsk), Russia

Died: January 21, 1924, in Gorki, Soviet Union (present-day Russia)

Wife: Nadezhda Krupskaya (married 1898-1924)

Children: None

In 1887, Vladimir Ulyanov began his studies at Kazan Imperial University in Kazan, Russia, to study law. While there, he was introduced to the ideas of Karl Marx, and he came to believe that Marxism (or communism) was the right form of government. Communism is a form of government created by Karl Marx and Friedrich Engels. In a communist system, citizens do not own anything because the government controls everything. During this time, Vladimir became involved in politics and revolutionary groups. In 1893, he left college and moved to St. Petersburg, Russia, and became a leader of his own Marxist group called the Bolsheviks. Bolshevik means "one of the majority" in Russian. Vladimir was a powerful speaker and knew how to get crowds excited about his ideas.

In late 1895, because of his dangerous and revolutionary ideas, Vladimir was put in prison by the Russian government but was later released and lived in exile in Siberia for three years. He continued his underground (secretive) communistic work and took the last name "Lenin" because he did not want people to figure out who he was or what he was doing. He began planning a revolution against the Russian government, which was led by Tsar (or Czar) Nicholas II at that time. Russia was suffering greatly due to a record number of deaths from World War I, and many of the remaining soldiers felt frustrated and hopeless. Also, the country's peasants (poor farmers) were suffering greatly from hunger and starvation due to the costly war efforts.

As a result of these things, in 1917, while World War I was still going on, the February Revolution occurred in Russia. The revolution was started by Russian peasants who were suffering financially and needed food. It lasted for eight days, and the Russian government under Tsar Nicholas II was overthrown. This marked the official end of the Russian Empire. Sadly, over 1,200 people were killed during these protests. Later in that same year, Lenin returned to Russia and led the Bolshevik Revolution to overthrow the new provisional (temporary) Russian government. He was successful and made himself the new ruler of Russia, which was renamed the Russian Socialist Federative Soviet Republic. Almost immediately, groups formed against Lenin's Bolshevik government, and a Russian civil war began.

During the Russian Civil War, Lenin brutally oppressed and mistreated the Russian people. He also created a plan of terror called War Communism, which gave control and ownership of everything to the government. It also allowed soldiers to take whatever they wanted or needed from the Russian people.

In 1922, after the Bolsheviks won the civil war, Lenin established the Soviet Union, the first communist country in the world. It combined fifteen separate nations into one very large country, called the Union of Soviet Socialist Republics (USSR). Vladimir Lenin was one of the most infamous, influential, and cruel world leaders in history.

Tsar Nicholas II of Russia

Vladimir Lenin speaking in Moscow, Russia, in 1920

INTERESTING FACT

Vladimir Lenin's wife, Nadezhda Krupskaya, was also a member of the Bolsheviks. She was an influential Soviet revolutionist (someone who wants to change the world, oftentimes by using violence).

Winston Churchill
1874 - 1965

Winston Churchill

Born: November 30, 1874, in Blenheim Palace, Oxfordshire, England

Died: January 24, 1965, at Kensington, London, England

Wife: Clementine Hozier (married 1908-1965)

Children: Diana, Randolph, Sarah, Marigold, Mary

From 1893-1894, Winston Churchill attended the Royal Military College in Sandhurst, England. While there, he trained to join the British cavalry, which is the division of the military in which soldiers ride on horses. After graduating from the Royal Military College, he became an officer in the 4th Queen's Own Hussars and later served in South Africa in the Second Boer War (1899-1902).

In 1900, Mr. Churchill was elected into his first government office when he became a member of the British Parliament. He was a member of the Conservative Party at first but then switched to the Liberal Party in 1904. During World War I (1914-1918), he served as the First Lord of the Admiralty and suffered a great military defeat when his British invasion of Gallipoli, Turkey, completely failed.

After World War I ended, Mr. Churchill continued in politics, and in 1924, he won a seat in the House of Commons, switching back to the Conservative Party. Throughout the 1930s, he began to warn his country about the German leader Adolf Hitler, who ultimately desired to take over and rule all of Europe. Most people, including British Prime Minister Neville Chamberlain, ignored Mr. Churchill's warnings. Prime Minister Chamberlain met with Hitler in an attempt to pursue peace and avoid another war (this is known as appeasement). They seemingly agreed to peace and signed the Munich Agreement. Thinking the meeting had been successful, Prime Minister Chamberlain returned to England, proclaiming that he had achieved peace with Hitler.

However, on September 1, 1939, Hitler broke his promise, invaded Poland, and officially began World War II. In May of 1940, Prime Minister Chamberlain resigned, and Mr. Churchill became the new British Prime Minister. He immediately started forming plans to defend his country against Hitler and the Germans.

Throughout World War II, Prime Minister Churchill's bravery and unwillingness to surrender to Hitler encouraged the British people and helped the Allies (the countries fighting against Germany) win World War II. He helped to prepare his country for the Battle of Britain (1940) and also eventually worked with United States President Franklin D. Roosevelt to help end World War II.

After the war ended in Europe, in July of 1945, Mr. Churchill was not reelected as Prime Minister. Some historians believe that he lost because the British people did not think that the man who had led them during wartime should be the one to lead them during peace-time. However, in 1951, he decided to run again and was elected a second time as Prime Minister for the Conservative Party. He served in that position until 1955.

In 1953, Prime Minister Churchill was knighted by Queen Elizabeth II, which means that he received the title "Sir" before his name. He continued to stay active in public life until his death in 1965.

Winston Churchill was one of the most famous, admired, and influential world leaders of all time.

Josef Stalin (left), Franklin D. Roosevelt (center), and Winston Churchill (right) at the 1943 Tehran Conference in Tehran, Iran, to discuss their strategy for defeating the Axis (Hitler and his allies)

FUN FACT

Winston Churchill was a prolific (active and accomplished) author of history books. In 1953, he received the Nobel Prize in Literature. Also, in 1963, he received honorary citizenship of the United States.

Josef Stalin
1878 – 1953

Josef Stalin

Born: December 18, 1878 (he claimed to have been born on December 21, 1879, for unknown reasons), in Gori, Georgia (a country that was part of the Russian Empire at that time)

Died: March 5, 1953, at his home, the Kuntsevo Dacha, in Moscow, present-day Russia

Wives: Ekaterina Svanidze (married 1906-1907), Nadezhda Alliluyeva (married 1919-1932)

Children: Yakov, Konstantin, Artyom (adopted), Vasily, Svetlana (Konstantin was born to a woman named Maria Kuzakova during the time between Stalin's two marriages.)

Iosif Vissarionovich Dzhugashvili (later known as Josef Stalin) attended the Tbilisi Spiritual Seminary in Georgia (near the border of Eastern Europe/Western Asia) to become a priest in the Russian Orthodox church. However, in 1899, he was expelled from the seminary because of his support of communism. Communism is a form of government created by Karl Marx and Friedrich Engels. In a communist system, citizens do not own anything because the government controls everything. After being expelled, Iosif joined the Bolshevik Party, which was led by a revolutionary communist named Vladimir Lenin. Stalin quickly became an important leader in the Bolshevik Party and organized riots, strikes, and bank robberies.

In 1917, the Bolsheviks took control of the Russian government during the Bolshevik Revolution. Stalin was given important positions in the new dictatorship, which is also a controlling and often cruel form of government. In 1922, he became the General Secretary of the Communist Party, and in 1929, he became the sole ruler of the newly formed Soviet Union after Vladimir Lenin's death.

Josef Stalin was one of the cruelest and most wicked leaders in history and was responsible for the death of over 20 million of his own Russian people, as well as thousands of people in other countries. If people did not agree with him and his government, he would often times purposely cause a famine in the area where they lived that would result in people dying from starvation. One of the most infamous killings that he orchestrated was called the Katyn Massacre in the spring of 1940. During this massacre, nearly 22,000 Polish military officers and citizens were killed.

In August of 1939, just before the start of World War II, Stalin signed a non-aggression pact with Adolf Hitler, the leader of Germany. This meant that both countries agreed to not attack each other. However, in mid-1941, Hitler violated (went against) the pact and invaded the Soviet Union. Because of this, Stalin joined the side of the Allies (Great Britain, United States, France, and others), which were the countries fighting against Hitler and his Nazi army. Near the end of 1941, the Nazis retreated out of the Soviet Union, and for the rest of the war, Stalin led the Soviet Army in pushing Hitler's army back into Germany.

After World War II ended in 1945, Stalin set up communist governments in many countries throughout Eastern Europe. This led to the beginning of the Cold War (1945-1991) between the Soviet Union and the United States. On March 5, 1953, Josef Stalin died and was eventually succeeded by Nikita Khrushchev. In 1956, Mr. Khrushchev denounced (publicly rejected) Stalin and began the de-Stalinization of the Soviet Union, hoping for more peaceful times.

Josef Stalin was one of the cruelest and most infamous communist leaders in history.

Josef Stalin (left) and Vladimir Lenin (right)

Russian soldiers defending Moscow during Adolf Hitler's invasion of the Soviet Union in 1941

INTERESTING FACT

While he was a member of the Bolshevik Party, Iosif Vissarionovich Dzhugashvili took the name Stalin, which means "man of steel" in Russian.

Albert Einstein
1879 – 1955

Albert Einstein

Born: March 14, 1879, in Ulm, Germany

Died: April 18, 1955, in Princeton, New Jersey

Wives: Mileva Maric (married 1903-1919), Elsa Einstein (Albert's second cousin; married 1919-1936)

Children: Lieserl, Hans, Eduard

As a young boy, Albert Einstein learned a lot about electronics and science from his father, Hermann. From 1896-1900, he attended the Swiss Federal Institute of Technology in Zurich, Switzerland, to learn more about math and science. After he graduated, Albert continued to think deeply about aspects of science, especially about the nature of space and light. In 1901, he published a paper on science called *Conclusions Drawn from the Phenomena of Capillarity*.

In 1902, Mr. Einstein got a job at the Swiss Patent Office, which is a place where people receive patents for their inventions. He worked at this job until 1909. During this time, Mr. Einstein continued to write hundreds of scientific papers, and he began to be recognized for his discoveries. He was offered a few different teaching positions at universities in Switzerland, Austria-Hungary, and Germany.

In 1905, Mr. Einstein published the theory of special relativity, which explored his ideas about space. It included the famous equation $E=mc^2$ that tells how to calculate the speed of light. In 1915, he published the theory of general relativity, which explains his ideas about gravity. These theories together are known as the theory of relativity, and they changed the way scientists look at the world. They also influenced the invention of nuclear weapons, including the atomic bomb, which was dropped by the United States on two Japanese cities during World War II.

In the early 1920s, Mr. Einstein traveled to many places around the world, lecturing to thousands of people and meeting many important leaders. His visits to countries like the United States, Japan, Palestine, and Spain helped to make him and his scientific accomplishments very well-known around the world.

In 1933, because he was a Jew, Mr. Einstein immigrated to the United States in order to escape the Nazis in Germany. The Nazis were a racist political group of Germans under the leadership of Adolf Hitler, who hated and supported the murder of millions of Jews simply because they were Jewish. In 1940, Mr. Einstein became an official citizen of the United States.

During World War II, Mr. Einstein wrote a letter to United States President Franklin D. Roosevelt to warn him of the possibility of Germany creating its own atomic bomb, which would have caused much destruction and death. This letter helped to change history because it prompted (caused) the United States government to get involved with nuclear research and development.

In addition to being a responsible United States citizen, Mr. Einstein was also a scholar at the Institute for Advanced Study at Princeton University in New Jersey from 1933 until his death in 1955. A scholar is someone who researches and becomes very knowledgeable about a particular subject and and then sometimes teaches about it.

Albert Einstein was one of the most famous and influential scientists of all time, and his important discoveries are studied all around the world today.

$E=mc^2$ sculpture in Berlin, Germany

Albert Einstein receiving American citizenship in 1940 from United States Third Circuit Judge Phillip Forman

FUN FACT

When he was young, Albert Einstein's teachers thought he was a slow learner because he was not interested in or good at several school subjects. Even if you have trouble with schoolwork, do not give up, work hard, and remember Mr. Einstein.

Pablo Picasso
1881 – 1973

Pablo Picasso

Born: October 25, 1881, in Málaga, Spain

Died: April 8, 1973, in Mougins, France

Wives: Olga Khokhlova (married 1918–1955), Jacqueline Roque (married 1961–1973)

Children: Paulo, Maya, Claude, Paloma (Maya was born to a woman named Marie-Thérèse Walter, and Claude and Paloma were born to a woman named Françoise Gilot.)

Pablo Picasso's father, José, was a painter and an art teacher. As a young boy, Pablo loved to draw and was not interested in school. He was a talented artist, and at the age of fourteen, he was accepted into the School of Fine Arts in Barcelona, Spain. Two years later, Pablo moved to Madrid (the capital of Spain) and attended the Royal Academy of San Fernando. However, Pablo was bored with the classical teachings of both of these schools, and he wanted to paint in a new way.

Mr. Picasso's artistic style went through several phases for the rest of his life. The first phase was the "Blue Period" (1901-1904). During this time, he painted pictures, such as *The Old Guitarist*, that were dominated by the color blue and depicted sad people.

Mr. Picasso's next phase was the "Rose Period" (1904-1906). During this time, he began to recover from a state of depression, and he painted pictures that were filled with brighter, happier colors like pink and red. One of his paintings during this time was *Mother and Child* (1901). He actually painted many different versions of it throughout his life, such as *Mother and child in front of a vase of flowers* (1901), *Mother and child on the shore* (1902), *Mother and Child* (1921), and *Mother and Child* (1965). Each painting had different figures and a unique look to it.

In 1907, Mr. Picasso and another artist named Georges Braque began to work on a new style of painting, called Cubism. They created this style in which something is painted from a specific viewpoint using geometric shapes like squares and triangles. An example of this style can be seen in Picasso's self-portrait (drawing of himself) that was done in 1907.

During the early 1920s, Picasso began to paint in the Neoclassical Style, which origianted (began) in the mid-1700s and was partly derived (came) from the work of Italian architect Andrea Palladio. One of Mr. Picasso's paintings in this style was *The Pipes of Pan* (1923). In 1924, he also began to use different ideas from the Surrealist movement in some of his paintings, such as *Guernica*, which was done in 1937 and is his most famous piece of art. *Guernica* depicts the suffering of people and animals affected by violence and is considered to be one of the most powerful anti-war paintings in art history.

Mr. Picasso continued to paint for the rest of his life, and he and his paintings became very popular around the world. Over the course of his life, he produced 1,885 paintings, 1,228 sculptures, and thousands of other types of artwork. Pablo Picasso was one of the most famous and influential artists of all time.

Mother and child in front of a vase of flowers *by Pablo Picasso*

Pablo Picasso with former U.S. President Harry Truman in Vallauris, France, in 1958

Guernica *by Pablo Picasso*

FUN FACT

Picasso's full name was Pablo Diego José Francisco de Paula Juan Nepomuceno María de los Remedios Cipriano de la Santísima Trinidad Ruiz y Picasso. Try saying that ten times fast!

Franklin D. Roosevelt
1882 - 1945

Franklin D. Roosevelt

Born: January 30, 1882, in Hyde Park, New York

Died: April 12, 1945, in Warm Springs, Georgia

Wife: Eleanor Roosevelt (married 1905-1945)

Children: Anna, James, Franklin Jr. (who died young), Elliot, Franklin Jr., John

In 1903, Franklin D. Roosevelt graduated from Harvard University in Massachusetts with a degree in history. He then went on to Columbia University in New York, where he studied until 1907.

In 1911, he began his political career when he was elected as a state senator in New York. Around this time, Mr. Roosevelt contracted a sickness called polio, which caused him to be paralyzed and have to use a wheelchair for the rest of his life. In 1914, he ran for a seat in the United States Senate but lost. In 1920, he ran as the vice presidential candidate for Democratic presidential nominee James Cox, but they lost the election to Warren G. Harding. Despite these losses, Mr. Roosevelt went on to become the governor of New York in 1929. Three years later, in 1932, he ran for president as a Democrat and won.

President Roosevelt wanted to help Americans during the Great Depression, which was a difficult time in which many businesses failed and people struggled to make money and keep their jobs. He formed a plan called the "New Deal," which gave government support and money to Americans. Even though the "New Deal" provided jobs for many Americans at that time, the Supreme Court ruled that six of President Roosevelt's "New Deal" plans were unconstitutional, which means that they went against the U.S. Constitution. In addition to the "New Deal," President Roosevelt was also well known for his radio addresses during the Great Depression, called "Fireside Chats," in which he tried to comfort the American people over the radio.

In 1936, Mr. Roosevelt was elected to a second term as president and continued with his "New Deal" plans. When World War II began in September of 1939, the United States passed the Neutrality Act of 1939, which declared that America would not take part in fighting against Nazi Germany and its allies (the Axis).

In 1940, President Roosevelt was elected to a third term, and this made him the first U.S. president to be elected more than two times. He was elected mainly because the American people were happy that he had kept them out of World War II. However, on December 7, 1941, Japan attacked America in Pearl Harbor, Hawaii. Because of this, President Roosevelt decided to enter America into the war.

World War II continued for four more years. During the war, President Roosevelt met with leaders of different countries, including British Prime Minister Winston Churchill, in order to stay involved in the war effort and defeat Adolf Hitler and his allies.

In 1944, President Roosevelt was elected as president for the fourth time. However, he never completed his term because he died in April of 1945, just a few months before World War II ended. Franklin D. Roosevelt was elected to four terms, more than any other president in American history. As a result of this, the 22nd Amendment to the United States Constitution was ratified in 1951, limiting all future presidents to two elected terms.

President Franklin D. Roosevelt was one of the most famous and popular world leaders of all time.

President Franklin D. Roosevelt with his dog, Fala, and a little girl named Ruthie Bie

President Franklin D. Roosevelt delivering a "Fireside Chat" in 1935

FUN FACT

Franklin D. Roosevelt had a dog named Fala, who became popular while Mr. Roosevelt was president. Sometimes, people would cut hairs off of Fala to keep as a souvenir.

Harry S. Truman
1884 - 1972

Harry S. Truman

Born: May 8, 1884, in Lamar, Missouri

Died: December 26, 1972, in Independence, Missouri

Wife: Elizabeth ("Bess") Wallace (married 1919-1972)

Children: Mary Margaret

Harry S. Truman served in the U.S. Army during World War I (1914-1918), and in 1922, he began his political career when he was elected as a judge on the Jackson County Court in Missouri. In 1934, he was elected as a United States Senator from Missouri and served as a senator for ten years. In 1944, when Franklin D. Roosevelt ran for president a third time, he chose Mr. Truman as his vice presidential candidate, and they won the election as the Democratic Party candidates. Several months later, in 1945, President Roosevelt died, which made Mr. Truman the next president.

During Mr. Truman's presidency, America was involved in three major wars: World War II (1939-1945), the Cold War (1945-1991), and the Korean War (1950-1953). (See my first book, *U.S. History Bites*, for more information on these three events). World War II was almost over when Mr. Truman became president. Even though Germany had surrendered, Japan had not. In order to end the war, President Truman was advised to attack Japan, so he ordered American bomber pilots to drop an atomic bomb on a city in Japan called Hiroshima. President Truman assumed this would cause the Japanese to surrender, but they did not. So, three days later, a second atomic bomb was dropped on the city of Nagasaki. These bombs were extremely dangerous and killed thousands of people. This act forced Japan to surrender, which finally ended World War II. The dropping of the atomic bombs began what is known as the Nuclear (or Atomic) Age.

During the Cold War, President Truman wanted certain countries to have their own free, democratic governments instead of being ruled by the communistic government of the Soviet Union. This policy is known as the Truman Doctrine and offered American support for nations threatened by Soviet communism. However, the Soviet Union, led by Josef Stalin at that time, rejected the Truman Doctrine and wanted countries to be communist instead.

During President Truman's second term, the Korean War began and then ended after he left office. During this war, in 1951, President Truman fired U.S. Army General Douglas MacArthur. General MacArthur was in command of the U.S. forces in Korea and had been the leader of the U.S. Army in the Pacific Ocean during World War II. President Truman fired him because he went against the orders and opinion of the president and his cabinet regarding a decision during the Korean War. Although many Americans were angry about General MacArthur's removal, President Truman believed that he had made the right decision based on the U.S. Constitution and that the military needed to take orders from the government and not the other way around.

After his presidency ended in 1953, Mr. Truman went on to write several books, including one called *Years of Trial and Hope*, which was about his time as president. Because of his presidency, involvement in three wars, and the atomic bombs, Harry S. Truman is known as one of the most famous and influential American presidents and world leaders in history.

President Harry Truman and General Douglas MacArthur

Smoke plume after the atomic bomb exploded on Nagasaki, Japan

FUN FACT

By the time he was fifteen years old, Harry Truman had read all of the books in his hometown library in Independence, Missouri, including many large volumes of encyclopedias.

Adolf Hitler
1889 - 1945

Adolf Hitler

Born: April 20, 1889, in Braunau am Inn, Austria

Died: April 30, 1945, in Berlin, Germany

Wife: Eva Braun (married for one day: April 29, 1945 – April 30, 1945)

Children: Unknown

Adolf Hitler served in the German army from 1914-1920 and fought in World War I. In 1919, he joined the German Worker's Party, which eventually became known as the National Socialist German Workers Party (Nazi Party for short). Hitler became an important leader in the party, and in 1924, he was put in prison for causing violence against the German government. While in prison, Hitler wrote an autobiography called *Mein Kampf* ("My Struggle"), which was about his personal life and racist ideas. Racism is believing that one race of people is better than another. Hitler's book, *Mein Kampf*, is full of hate toward Jewish people and other nations that he believed needed to either be defeated or eliminated. He was released from prison in December of 1924, and *Mein Kampf* was published in 1925.

In 1933, Hitler became the Chancellor of Germany. The office of chancellor was similar to the position of the Prime Minister of Great Britain.

After German President Paul von Hindenburg died in 1934, Hitler took complete control of the German government, becoming its dictator. He was a cruel leader, and he attacked and killed people who did not support the Nazi government. He was called the "Führer," which means "leader" in German.

Hitler believed that the greatest race of humankind was the Aryan, or white German, race. He saw other races as inferior (less than) the Aryan race and was responsible for the killing of millions of non-German people, particularly Jews. By the time Hitler died, the Nazi government had murdered over six million Jewish men, women, and children in an event called The Holocaust.

In 1939, Hitler started World War II when his army invaded Poland. The Nazi military (known as The Wehrmacht) was divided into three main groups: the Heer (army/land soldiers), the Kriegsmarine (navy), and the Luftwaffe (air force). Hitler had many Nazi generals under his command, including Hermann Göering and Erwin Rommel.

Following their successful invasion of Poland, the Nazis took over much of Europe, including Denmark, Norway, and France. Hitler also tried to conquer Great Britain and the Soviet Union but was unsuccessful because of brave men like British Prime Minister Winston Churchill and others.

During World War II, the Axis were the side led by Adolf Hitler (Germany), Benito Mussolini (Italy), and Emperor Hirohito (Japan). The Allies included the countries of Great Britain, the United States, and France, and they fought against the Axis. In June of 1944, the Allies carried out a plan called the D-Day invasion against the Nazis on the Normandy beaches in France. As a result of this successful attack, Germany eventually lost all of the land it had conquered during the war.

At the end of April of 1945, Hitler killed himself in Berlin, Germany, as the Soviet Army was taking control of the city. Adolf Hitler is known for being an evil leader who was responsible for the death of millions of people.

Adolf Hitler with his Nazi staff in 1940
(He is wearing black pants)

British forces landing on the Normandy beaches on D-Day

Wall of Remembrance at the U.S. National Holocaust Museum

INTERESTING FACT

Adolf Hitler had a pet cat named Schnitzel. Schnitzel is a type of meat that is breaded and fried, and it is a traditional German meal.

Agatha Christie
1890 - 1976

Agatha Christie

Born: September 15, 1890, in Torquay, Devon, England

Died: January 12, 1976, at her home, Winterbrook House, in Wallingford, Oxfordshire, England

Husbands: Archibald Christie (married 1914-1928), Max Mallowan (married 1930-1976)

Children: Rosalind

As a young girl, Agatha Christie's mother, Clarissa, used to tell her stories at bedtime each night, and Agatha taught herself how to read when she was only five years old. She also used to make up her own stories, using her pets and dolls as characters.

Agatha loved reading mystery/detective novels. She especially liked the books of Wilkie Collins, such as *The Woman in White*. She also enjoyed and was inspired by the stories of the famous detective Sherlock Holmes, which were written by a man named Sir Arthur Conan Doyle.

In 1920, Mrs. Christie published her first book, *The Mysterious Affair at Styles*, which was a mystery novel. In it, she introduced her most famous detective, named Hercule Poirot. She published more mystery novels in the 1920s, including *The Murder of Roger Ackroyd* (1926). These books helped to make her very famous in America and throughout parts of Europe.

In late 1926, Mrs. Christie's first husband, Archibald Christie, wanted to get a divorce (they divorced two years later). On the night of December 3, 1926, after her husband had left to visit a friend, Mrs. Christie left their home in Surrey, England, and disappeared for ten days. Thousands of police officers and volunteers searched for her. On December 14th, she was found at the Swan Hydropathic Hotel in Yorkshire, England. No one knows exactly why she disappeared. Some people believe that she left because she was so depressed from her exhausting work, the death of her mother that year, and her husband wanting to leave her for another woman. A movie was made about her strange disappearance, called *Agatha*, which was released in 1979 after her death.

In 1930, Ms. Christie published *Murder at the Vicarage*, which many people believe is her best book. She published several more books throughout the 1930s, including *Murder on the Orient Express* (1934) and *And Then There Were None* (1939), both of which are also murder mysteries. *And Then There Were None* has sold over 100 million copies around the world and is her best-selling book.

In addition to over seventy books, Ms. Christie also wrote many plays, including *Witness for the Prosecution* and *The Mousetrap*, which still plays today and has been performed tens of thousands of times.

Since her death, Agatha Christie has become one of the best-selling authors of all time (over two billion sales), and she is known as "The Queen of Mystery." Her books have been translated into over 100 languages, and many movies and TV series have been made based on her books.

Agatha Christie at the Acropolis in Athens, Greece, in 1958

Agatha Christie at her typewriter

The Mousetrap by Agatha Christie playing at St. Martin's Theatre in London, England

FUN FACT

Agatha Christie and her second husband, Max Mallowan, were reportedly some of the first English people to ever try surfing. Prince Edward VIII was the first person to try it.

Dwight D. Eisenhower
1890 – 1969

Dwight D. Eisenhower

Born: October 14, 1890, in Denison, Texas

Died: March 28, 1969, in Washington, D.C., United States

Wife: Marie ("Mamie") Doud (married 1916-1969)

Children: Doud, John

Dwight D. Eisenhower was born in Texas, but he grew up in Kansas as the third of seven boys in a poor family. In 1911, he entered the United States Military Academy of West Point in New York and graduated from there in 1915. While there, Dwight was trained how to be a soldier, and he also developed his leadership skills.

During World War I (1914-1918), Captain Eisenhower's job was to train officer candidates for the U.S. Army. Even though he did not get to fight in the war himself, Mr. Eisenhower knew that his job was important.

Between World War I and World War II, Mr. Eisenhower had many important positions in the military, and he traveled throughout the United States, the Panama Canal Zone, and the Philippines. He was an aide (assistant) to important leaders like General John J. Pershing, who led the U.S. Army during World War I, and General Douglas MacArthur, who went on to lead the U.S. Army in the Pacific Ocean during World War II.

Mr. Eisenhower continued to promote in rank in the military and was beloved by many people as one of the greatest United States officers. Before America entered World War II near the end of 1941, he was promoted to the rank of brigadier general and served as the chief of staff for a few different divisions of the U.S. Army.

During World War II, General Eisenhower advanced to become the Supreme Commander of the Allied Expeditionary Force. He made many important decisions during World War II about how America should fight Nazi Germany and its allies (the Axis), including the strategies used for D-Day in 1944. On June 6, 1944, America and its allies (the Allies) captured the Normandy beaches in France, which were held by the Axis. From there, they took back a lot of land in Europe from the Germans that had been lost during the war. After World War II ended in 1945, Mr. Eisenhower returned home a hero, and he had become a five-star general.

In 1952, Mr. Eisenhower decided to run for president as a Republican and won the election in a landslide. His accomplishments as president included helping to end the Korean War (1950-1953) and setting up NASA (National Aeronautics and Space Administration). He also helped to establish the U.S. Highway System and fought against segregation. Segregation was when black people were separated from white people because of their skin color and were not allowed to participate in or enjoy the same benefits as white people.

After his presidency ended, Mr. Eisenhower spent his retirement golfing and writing. One of his books, *Mandate for Change*, was about his time as president.

Dwight D. Eisenhower was a very popular United States president and is considered to be one of the greatest American generals of all time.

General Dwight D. Eisenhower talking to D-Day troops

Dwight D. Eisenhower campaigning for president in 1952
("Ike" was his nickname from an early age)

FUN FACT

In 1955, during Dwight D. Eisenhower's presidency, Disneyland opened in Anaheim, California.

J.R.R. Tolkien
1892 - 1973

J.R.R. Tolkien

Born: January 3, 1892, in Bloemfontein, South Africa

Died: September 2, 1973, in Bournemouth, England

Wife: Edith Bratt (married 1916-1971)

Children: John, Michael, Christopher, Priscilla

John Ronald Reuel (J.R.R.) Tolkien's father, Arthur, worked for the Bank of Africa in South Africa, and he lived there with his wife, Mabel. In 1895, Mabel took their two sons, John Ronald and Hilary, back to England, where she had lived before moving to South Africa with her husband. Arthur Tolkien planned to finish up some business at the bank and join them in England later, but sadly, he died the following year in 1896 while still in South Africa.

Mabel Tolkien was very sad after her husband died, but she worked hard to raise her two sons well. John Ronald developed an interest in ancient languages when he was young because his mother taught him Greek and Latin at home. He attended King Edward's Grammar School in Birmingham, England, as a child and went on to Oxford University when he was older. After Mabel died in 1904, a Catholic priest named Father Francis Morgan looked after John Ronald and Hilary.

John Ronald loved philology, which is the study of languages, and he invented some of his own languages. He was also interested in and inspired by Norse mythology and eventually created his own mythology based on his invented languages. Tolkien's imaginary world is called Middle-earth, and he wrote many stories about it throughout the rest of his life.

After graduating from Oxford in 1915, Mr. Tolkien served in World War I (1914-1918), during which two of his closest friends died. After serving in the war, he contributed work for the *Oxford English Dictionary* from 1918-1920 and taught English Language at Leeds University from 1920-1925. In 1925, Mr. Tolkien became a professor at Oxford University, where he taught Anglo-Saxon and Old and Middle English until his retirement in 1959. He was good friends with the future famous author C.S. Lewis, and they were part of a writer's group called the Inklings, who met regularly twice a week in Oxford.

In 1937, Mr. Tolkien published *The Hobbit*, which was his first published tale that took place in Middle-earth. In 1954 and 1955, he published *The Lord of the Rings*, which is made up of three individual books: *The Fellowship of the Ring*, *The Two Towers*, and *The Return of the King*. Both *The Hobbit* and *The Lord of the Rings* have sold hundreds of millions of copies around the world and have been translated into many different languages. They are some of the most-loved works of fiction of all time, and six very popular films have been made based on them.

After his retirement from Oxford University in 1959, Mr. Tolkien spent the last years of his life writing and publishing a few more books and relaxing with his wife, Edith. He also worked on finishing another book called *The Silmarillion*, which was published in 1977 after his death.

J.R.R. Tolkien is beloved around the world today as one of the greatest authors of all time. (See my book *J.R.R. Tolkien History Bites* for more information on him.)

The Eagle and Child pub, where the Inklings met

J.R.R. Tolkien in his office at Merton College, Oxford University in 1955

FUN FACT

J.R.R. Tolkien was a devout Catholic. He once said that the purpose of life "is to increase according to our capacity our knowledge of God by all means we have, and to be moved by it to praise and thanks."

Mao Zedong
1893 - 1976

Mao Zedong

Born: December 26, 1893, in Shaoshan, Hunan province, China

Died: September 9, 1976, in Beijing, China

Wives: Luo Yixiu (married 1907-1910), Yang Kaihui (married 1920-1930), He Zizhen (married 1930-1937), Jiang Qing (married 1938-1976)

Children: Mao Anying, Mao Anqing, Mao Anlong, Yang, Mao Anhong, Li Min, Li Na (He also had two sons and one daughter whose names are unknown.)

As a young man, Mao Zedong was rebellious against his father, Mao Yichang, who was a peasant farmer in China. In 1911, during the Chinese Revolution, Mao (Zedong) joined the rebel army, which was fighting against the Qing dynasty, who ruled China at that time. In 1921, he became a communist and was an important leader in the Communist Party. Communism is a form of government created by Karl Marx and Friedrich Engels. In a communist system, citizens do not own anything because the government controls everything.

Around this time, the Chinese Nationalist Party became allies with the Chinese Communist Party, and Mao went to work for President Sun Yat-sen of China. In 1925, President Sun Yat-sen died, and Chiang Kai-shek, who was a Nationalist, became the new leader of China. He separated the Nationalists and Communists and began to kill and imprison leaders of the Communist Party. This led to the Chinese Civil War (first stage: 1927-1937; second stage: 1945-1949).

In 1934, President Kai-shek led an army of about one million men to destroy the communists, but Mao Zedong led thousands of the communists south on what is called the Long March. They journeyed over 7,000 miles in southern China and then moved north to the Shaanxi province.

After World War II ended in 1945, Mao led an army of Communists against Chiang Kai-shek and the Nationalists and eventually defeated them in 1949. Mao founded the People's Republic of China, and he ruled over it as the Chairman of the Communist Party. He was a harsh and cruel leader and was responsible for the deaths of millions of his own people who did not agree with or support him.

In 1958, Mao created a new government plan called the Great Leap Forward, which was supposed to help China's agricultural and economic (money) systems. Instead, it caused a horrible famine that led to millions of Chinese people starving to death. This terrible situation caused Mao to lose absolute control of the government for a time. However, in 1966, he returned to power again during the Cultural Revolution, which was supported by many young peasants.

Mao Zedong was one of the cruelest leaders of all time and one of the most infamous communists in history. One thing that he is well-known for is his book of quotes, called *The Little Red Book* or *Quotations from Chairman Mao* (1964). Around two billion copies of it were distributed throughout China during his rule, and citizens were required to carry it around with them wherever they went.

Mao Zedong in front of a crowd in China

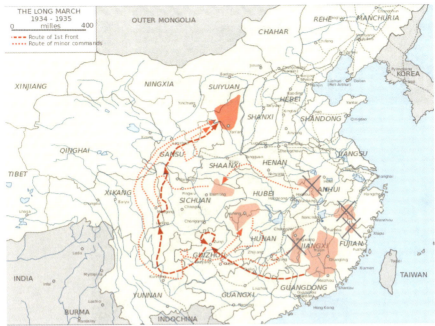

Map of the Long March of 1934-1935

INTERESTING FACT

Mao Zedong was a prolific (active and accomplished) poet. Some of his poems relate to famous events in his life, such as "The Long March." Other poems of his include "Changsha" (1925), "Snow" (1936), and "The PLA Captures Nanjing" (1949).

Babe Ruth
1895 – 1948

Babe Ruth

Born: February 6, 1895, in Baltimore, Maryland

Died: August 16, 1948, in New York City, New York

Wives: Helen Woodford (married 1914-1929), Claire Merritt (married 1929-1948)

Children: Julia, Dorothy

As a young boy, George Herman Ruth played a lot of baseball with children in his neighborhood. In 1902, because he was a very rebellious and misbehaving child, his parents sent him to St. Mary's Industrial School for Boys in Baltimore, Maryland, where he lived for twelve years. While there, one of the Brothers (Catholic men who worked there), Matthias Boutlier, helped George to improve his baseball skills.

George began to do so well in baseball that Jack Dunn hired him to play for the Baltimore Orioles, a minor league baseball team. While on this team, George got the nickname "Babe," and it stuck for the rest of his life.

In 1914, Babe began to play as a pitcher for the Boston Red Sox, but he later became a batter and hit many home runs. He was an excellent player, and he helped the Red Sox win three World Series (1915, 1916, and 1918).

In 1920, Mr. Ruth was traded to the New York Yankees baseball team, and he quickly became very popular because of his amazing batting abilities. "The Sultan of Swat," as he was called, helped the Yankees win four World Series, which was a very big accomplishment (1923, 1927, 1928, and 1932). During his career, Babe Ruth hit a total of 714 home runs and set many new records for the game.

In 1935, Mr. Ruth retired from playing baseball. He wanted to become the manager of a major league baseball team but was never hired. He also wanted to become a radio broadcaster for baseball games but was not hired for that job either. Mr. Ruth spent the rest of his retirement traveling and speaking, and he even acted in a film called *The Pride of the Yankees* with Gary Cooper (1942). A few weeks before he died of cancer, he attended the premier (opening) of a movie about his life, called *The Babe Ruth Story* (1948).

Babe Ruth is considered by many people to have been the world's greatest baseball player, and his sports career has inspired athletes around the world.

Babe Ruth pitching for the Red Sox in 1918

Babe Ruth batting for the New York Yankees around 1921

Gary Cooper (left) and Babe Ruth (right) acting in the movie The Pride of the Yankees

FUN FACT

Babe Ruth was friends with another famous baseball player named Lou Gehrig. Also, some people believe that the Baby Ruth candy bar is named after him. However, it is actually named after Ruth Cleveland, who was the oldest daughter of U.S. President Grover Cleveland.

Amelia Earhart
1897 - 1937

Amelia Earhart

Born: July 24, 1897, in Atchison, Kansas

Died: The exact date of her death is unknown. She disappeared on July 2, 1937, while flying over the Pacific Ocean, but was declared dead on January 5, 1939.

Husband: George P. Putnam (married 1931-1937)

Children: She had no biological children, but she had two stepsons, David and George Jr.

When Amelia Earhart was seven years old, she created a homemade roller coaster, which first introduced her to the feeling of flying. In 1908, while at the Iowa State Fair, she saw one of the Wright Brothers' airplanes but was not very interested in flying yet. In 1919, Amelia watched a World War I pilot fly a small plane, and it sparked in her a desire to fly.

Amelia flew as a passenger for the first time in 1920, and one year later, she took flying lessons from a female pilot named Anita Snook. Amelia soon bought her first plane and called it "The Canary." In 1923, she became the sixteenth woman ever to receive a pilot's license.

As a pilot, Ms. Earhart set many records, including being the first woman to fly solo (alone) across the Atlantic Ocean in 1932. Ms. Earhart became very famous for her flying achievements, and in 1932, she became the first woman to ever receive the Distinguished Flying Cross, which is an award from the United States Congress. Interestingly, in 1935, she also became the first pilot to fly solo from Honolulu, Hawaii, to Oakland, California.

In 1937, Ms. Earhart began a flight from Miami, Florida, over Africa, Asia, and onto New Guinea. She flew with her navigator, Fred Noonan, and wanted to become the first woman to fly around the world. On their way to Howland Island in the Pacific Ocean from New Guinea, they lost radio contact with the U.S. Coast Guard, disappeared, and were never seen or heard from again. No one knows what happened to them, but some people think that their plane ran out of fuel and crashed into the Pacific Ocean. Other people think that they were captured by the Japanese. Their plane and remains have never been found. Ms. Earhart's mysterious disappearance caused her to become even more famous, and it continues to interest many people today.

Amelia Earhart was one of the most famous pilots of all time and is well known around the world for her many accomplishments. She is also remembered for speaking out in favor of women's rights.

Anita Snook

Amelia Earhart's Lockheed Model 10-E Electra, the plane that she and Fred Noonan were lost in

Amelia Earhart and Fred Noonan

FUN FACT

Amelia Earhart was friends with First Lady Eleanor Roosevelt, who was the wife of U.S. President Franklin D. Roosevelt. Ms. Earhart helped to teach Mrs. Roosevelt how to fly, and the First Lady eventually earned a student's pilot license.

C.S. Lewis
1898 - 1963

C.S. Lewis

Born: November 29, 1898, in Belfast, Northern Ireland

Died: November 22, 1963, at his home, The Kilns, Oxford, England

Wife: Helen Joy Davidman Gresham (married 1956-1960)

Children: He had no biological children, but he adopted his two stepsons, David and Douglas.

Clive Staples Lewis was raised in a Christian home by his parents, Albert and Flora, but he became an atheist (someone who does not believe in the existence of God) during his teenage years. He grew up in Ireland and attended a couple different schools in England, including Wynyard School in Hertfordshire and Malvern College in Worcestershire.

Clive (who was known as "Jack" to his family and close friends) served in World War I (1914-1918), and during this war, his friend Edward "Paddy" Moore was killed. Before the war, the two young men had made a promise to look after each other's relatives if either of them was killed during the war. In keeping with this promise, after World War I, Clive took care of Paddy's mother, Janie, and younger sister, Maureen, and he watched out for them for many years. They lived with him and his older brother, Warren, at The Kilns, which was their home in Oxford, England.

In 1925, Mr. Lewis became a Fellow of Magdalen College at Oxford University. While there, he became good friends with the future famous author J.R.R. Tolkien, and they were part of a writer's group called the Inklings. Mr. Lewis served as a tutor of English Language and Literature at Oxford until 1954 when he took a position at Cambridge University as the Professor of Medieval and Renaissance English.

In 1930, Mr. Lewis became a theist, which is someone who believes in the existence of God. He then became a Christian in 1931 after having a conversation with two friends, J.R.R. Tolkien and Hugo Dyson, along Addison's Walk in Oxford.

Mr. Lewis went on to publish many famous books about Christianity throughout his life, including *The Problem of Pain* (1940), *The Screwtape Letters* (1942), *The Abolition of Man* (1943), *The Great Divorce* (1945), and *Mere Christianity* (1952). Also, during World War II, he gave a few series of broadcast talks for the BBC (British Broadcasting Corporation) about Christianity that were heard by millions of English people.

Between the years of 1950-1956, Mr. Lewis published the seven books in his series *The Chronicles of Narnia*, which have sold over 100 million copies worldwide and have been translated into dozens of languages. They are (in order of publication): *The Lion, the Witch, and the Wardrobe* (1950), *Prince Caspian* (1951), *The Voyage of the Dawn Treader* (1952), *The Silver Chair* (1953), *The Horse and His Boy* (1954), *The Magician's Nephew* (1955), and *The Last Battle* (1956). Also, three successful films have been made based on the first three Narnia books.

In 1952, Mr. Lewis met an American woman named Helen Joy Davidman Gresham. They had been writing letters back and forth to each other for two years. Eventually, they fell in love and got married in 1956. Sadly, however, after only a few years of marriage, Joy died of cancer in 1960. Mr. Lewis was very sad and angry at God at first. However, he said that his Christian faith became stronger when he realized that God had a purpose in Joy's death. Around this time, in 1961, Mr. Lewis published *A Grief Observed*, which described his great sadness over losing his wife.

C.S. Lewis was one of the most famous and influential Christian apologists and authors of all time.

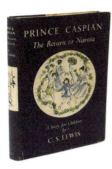 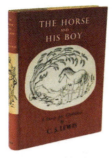  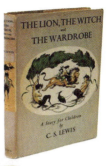
 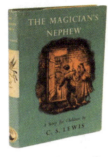 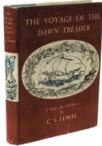

First editions of the seven books in **The Chronicles of Narnia** series

FUN FACT

C.S. Lewis saw Disney's Snow White and the Seven Dwarfs in theaters with J.R.R. Tolkien when it first came out in the United Kingdom in 1938.

Walt Disney
1901 - 1966

Walt Disney

Born: December 5, 1901, in Chicago, Illinois

Died: December 15, 1966, in Burbank, California

Wife: Lillian Bounds (married 1925-1966)

Children: Diane, Sharon

As a young boy, Walt Disney had an interest in art and studied it at McKinley High School in Chicago, Illinois. During World War I (1914-1918), he volunteered with the Red Cross Ambulance Corps in France. After he returned home, in 1921, he founded a company called Laugh-O-Grams and created his first cartoons. Many of his cartoons were based on well-known fairytales, such as *Little Red Riding Hood*, *Jack and the Beanstalk*, and *Goldie Locks and the Three Bears*. However, Walt's business did not end up making enough money to support itself, and because of this, he had to declare bankruptcy (which means he ran out of money). He packed up his things and moved to Hollywood, California.

While in Hollywood, in 1923, he founded the Disney Brothers Cartoon Studio with his younger brother, Roy. It was also called The Walt Disney Studio and Walt Disney Productions. Mr. Disney continued to make cartoons, such as the *Alice Comedies*, and draw cartoon characters. His most famous character was Mickey Mouse.

Mickey Mouse was first drawn by Mr. Disney and his friend Ubbe "Ub" Iwerks in 1928 for a short film called *Steamboat Willie*. Since then, Mickey Mouse has become one of the most popular and recognizable cartoon characters of all time.

In 1932, Mr. Disney created and released the first color cartoon movie in history, *Flowers and Trees*. It was eight minutes long and won an Academy Award for Best Animated Short Film. In 1937, The Walt Disney Studio released the first full-length cartoon movie, called *Snow White and the Seven Dwarfs*. It made millions of dollars around the world and quickly made Mr. Disney and his company very popular. During his lifetime, he created several other cartoon films, including *Pinocchio* (1940) and *Cinderella* (1950). Also, in 1955, Dinseyland opened in Anaheim, California.

Since his death, The Walt Disney Studio (renamed The Walt Disney Company in 1986 and now includes four divisions, one of which is Walt Disney Studios) has made almost 150 movies and billions of dollars worldwide. In 1971, under the direction of Walt's younger brother, Roy, Disney World opened in Orlando, Florida. Millions of people around the world have visited Disney World every year since.

Walt Disney was one of the most famous and influential artists and filmmakers of all time.

Statue of Walt Disney and Mickey Mouse in the Magic Kingdom, one of the four amusement parks of Disney World in Orlando, Florida

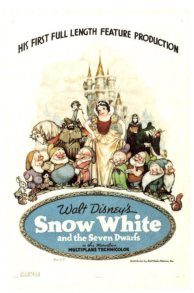

Original 1937 *Snow White and the Seven Dwarfs* movie poster

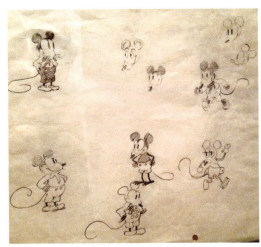

Earliest known drawings of Mickey Mouse by Walt Disney

FUN FACT

Walt Disney originally named his famous cartoon character "Mortimer Mouse," but his wife, Lillian, suggested that his first name should be "Mickey" instead.

George Orwell
1903 – 1950

George Orwell

Born: June 25, 1903, in Motihari, Bengal, India

Died: January 21, 1950, in London, England

Wives: Eileen O'Shaughnessy (married 1936-1945), Sonia Brownell (married 1949-1950)

Children: He had no biological children, but he adopted a boy named Richard with his first wife, Eileen.

Eric Blair's father, Richard, worked for the Indian Civil Service. It was an organization run by the British government in India because at that time in history, India was still part of the British Empire. In 1904, Eric's mother, Ida, took him and his two sisters to England, where her husband, Richard, and his family were from. Ida and her children settled in Oxfordshire, but Richard stayed in India, and the family did not see each other again until eight years later in 1912.

Eric grew up reading the works of Charles Dickens, William Shakespeare, and Rudyard Kipling. He was inspired by their writings to become an author himself one day. He attended a few different schools in England, and while in his late teens, he was tutored by men such as A.S.F. Gow, who was an English classical scholar and teacher, and Aldous Huxley, who was a famous English philosopher.

Despite his academic abilities, Eric's family could not afford to send him to a university. Since he was interested in the Far East and countries in Asia, his family encouraged him to join the Indian Imperial Police, which was the British police system in India at that time. Eric decided to join, and in 1922, he sailed to Burma (present-day Myanmar), which was a part of British India at that time, to become a policeman there. Eric had many adventures in India, and these adventures inspired his writing later on, including his novel *Burmese Days* (1934). In 1927, he returned home to England, and the next year, in 1928, he moved to Paris, France. He then moved back to England in December of 1929 and lived in London.

In 1933, Mr. Blair published his first book, *Down and Out in Paris and London* under the pen (fake) name "George

Orwell." *Down and Out in Paris and London* was about his memories of the sufferings of the poor people he saw while living in those two cities. Around this time, he also wrote articles and essays about socialism, which is a form of government in which businesses are owned by the community as a whole and not by individual business owners. Socialism is the phase of government between capitalism and communism. Mr. Orwell's essays about socialism became very influential in politics.

Out of a desire to fight against fascism (a form of government run by a dictator) in Spain, Mr. Orwell decided to go to Barcelona, Spain, in 1936 to fight in the Spanish Civil War (1936-1939). While there, he became a revolutionary socialist, which means that he believed the people of a country should rebel against their government, overthrow it, and become socialist. During the war, he was shot and nearly killed. After his time in the war, Mr. Orwell published *Homage to Catalonia*, a personal account of his experiences while fighting for the Republican army during the Spanish Civil War. In 1937, he moved back to England, and he lived in the United Kingdom for the rest of his life.

Near the end of World War II in 1945, Mr. Orwell published *Animal Farm*, which is an allegorical book that talks about the dangers of communism. In 1949, his book, *1984* was published, and in it, Mr. Orwell predicted that government would continue to control more of people's lives as time went on.

George Orwell was one of the most famous and influential English authors and political thinkers of all time. His books have sold millions of copies around the world and have been translated into dozens of languages.

George Orwell (holding a puppy) in 1937 during the Spanish Civil War

FUN FACT

George Orwell coined (invented) the term "Cold War" to describe the conflict between the United States and Russia after World War II. (See my first book, *U.S. History Bites*, for more information on this event.) Mr. Orwell first used the term in an essay published in 1945 called "You and the Atomic Bomb."

Mother Teresa
1910 – 1997

Mother Teresa

Born: August 26, 1910, in Üsküb (present-day Skopje, the capital of Macedonia), Yugoslavia (which was part of the Ottoman Empire at that time)

Died: September 5, 1997, in Calcutta, India

Husband: None

Children: None

Agnes Gonxha Bojaxhiu was raised in the Roman Catholic Church in Üsküb, Ottoman Empire (present-day Macedonia). When she was young, she decided to devote her life to serving God. At the age of eighteen, she joined the Sisters of Loreto, a group of Catholic women dedicated to spiritual education and helping the poor and struggling. Agnes spent one year in Ireland, where she learned how to speak English at the Loreto Abbey in the village of Rathfarnham, Ireland. It was here that she changed her name to Sister Mary Teresa.

In 1929, Mary traveled to India to become a missionary. She started her work as a missionary one year later in the town of Darjeeling, India, and was a teacher at the local school there. In 1931, she took her vows to become a nun. After this, she was sent to Calcutta, India, and was assigned to teach at Saint Mary's High School, where she eventually became headmistress. During her time at this school, she also learned Bengali and Hindi, two of the main languages of India.

In 1946, Mary believed she was called by God to help the poor and sick people in India. The next year, she took her Final Profession of Vows, in which she promised to live a life of poverty, chastity, and obedience. She also took the title of "Mother." She left Saint Mary's High School and went out among the poor Indian people of Calcutta, helping to feed the sick and starving even though she was very hungry most of the time herself and had to beg for food.

In 1950, Mother Teresa founded the Missionaries of Charity, a Catholic group dedicated to helping the poor and needy. Since then, this group has grown to include thousands of members all around the world.

Throughout the 1960s, Mother Teresa and her efforts to help the poor were recognized by people like Pope Paul VI, who awarded the Missionaries of Charity the Decree of Praise. Malcom Muggeridge also wrote a book and made a documentary about her. In 1979, she received the Nobel Peace Prize and a banquet was going to be thrown in her honor. However, she asked that the money for the banquet be donated to poor people in India instead. She continued to serve the poor, sick, and dying right up until her death.

Mother Teresa is remembered all around the world today for her great efforts to help the poor and needy. In 2016, she was canonized (made a saint) by the Roman Catholic Church.

The slums of Calcutta, India, where Mother Teresa served the poorest of the poor

Mother Teresa and Pope John Paul II in 1986

U.S. President Ronald Reagan, Mother Teresa, and Nancy Reagan at the White House (See "Fun Fact" below)

FUN FACT

In 1985, Mother Teresa received the Presidential Medal of Freedom from U.S. President Ronald Reagan at the White House. In her acceptance speech she quoted Jesus's words in Matthew 25:40, "...whatever you did for one of the least of these brothers and sisters of mine, you did for Me."

Ronald Reagan
1911 - 2004

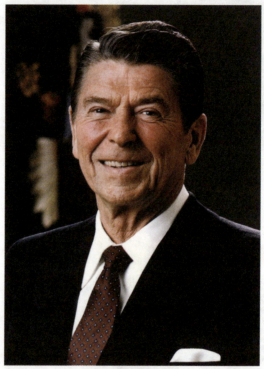

Ronald Reagan

Born: February 6, 1911, in Tampico, Illinois

Died: June 5, 2004, at his home in Los Angeles, California

Wives: Jane Wyman (married 1940-1949), Nancy Davis (married 1952-2004)

Children: Maureen, Michael (adopted), Patti, Ron Jr.

Throughout his childhood in the 1920s, Ronald Reagan and his family suffered during the Great Depression. After high school, he attended Eureka College and was the captain of the swim team. After college, he became a sports broadcaster and was a radio announcer for many different sporting events.

In 1937, Mr. Reagan became an actor and moved to Hollywood, California. He was the star (main character) in over fifty movies. One of his most famous movies is called *Knute Rockne: All American* (1940).

During World War II (1939-1945), Mr. Reagan served in the U.S. Army. Even though he could not fight because of his poor eyesight, he stayed back in America to make training movies for the Army.

In 1964, a Republican named Barry Goldwater ran for president. Mr. Reagan made many speeches to help him get elected, but Mr. Goldwater lost. However, these speeches made Mr. Reagan well known throughout America, and some people wanted him to run for president.

In 1966, Mr. Reagan was elected as governor of California and served eight years in this position. In 1976, he ran for president but lost the Republican nomination to Gerald Ford. However, four years later, in 1980, Mr. Reagan ran again, and this time, he won the election against President Jimmy Carter. A few months after he was elected, President Reagan was shot by a man named John Hinckley Jr. Thankfully, President Reagan survived and recovered in a few weeks.

Throughout his presidency, Mr. Reagan worked hard to improve the U.S. economy. His economic plan created 16 million new jobs, lowered taxes, and was referred to as "Reaganomics."

In 1984, President Reagan ran for a second term against Walter Mondale and won every single state except Minnesota. He won the most electoral college votes in any presidential election in U.S. history (525 out of a possible 538). When someone wins an election by a large margin, it is called a landslide victory.

During his second term in office, President Reagan worked with Soviet leader Mikhail Gorbachev to help end the Cold War (1945-1991) and also to eliminate many dangerous weapons called missiles. In 1987, the two leaders signed the INF Treaty, in which America and the Soviet Union agreed to destroy large amounts of their nuclear weapons. Also, mainly because of President Reagan and Gorbachev's work, the Berlin Wall was torn down in Europe, and this symbolized the end of communism there.

Ronald Reagan was one of the most famous and beloved American presidents and world leaders in history.

President Ronald Reagan and Queen Elizabeth II riding horses in 1982 at Windsor Castle in Berkshire, England

President Ronald Reagan and Mikhail Gorbachev in Iceland in 1986 for the the Reykjavik Summit to discuss the elimination of nuclear weapons

FUN FACT

Ronald Reagan loved jelly beans. When he became president, he bought over 6,000 pounds of blueberry-flavored ones.

Lucille Ball
1911 – 1989

Lucille Ball

Born: August 6, 1911, in Jamestown, New York

Died: April 26, 1989, in Los Angeles, California

Husbands: Desi Arnaz (married 1940-1960), Gary Morton (married 1961-1989)

Children: Lucie, Desi Jr.

Lucille Ball had a very difficult childhood. When she was just four years old, her father, Henry, died, and her mother, Desiree, married another man named Ed Peterson four years later. Lucy (as she was called) lived with Mr. Peterson's parents for a while, and she later described her time with them as miserable. During this time, she tried to escape her sadness by living in her imagination. When she was fifteen, Lucy went to the John Murray Anderson School for the Dramatic Arts in New York City to learn about acting on stage.

In 1927, Lucy became a model (someone who poses for pictures), and she worked for a fashion designer and a cigarette company. In the early 1930s, she moved to Hollywood, California, where her talents were recognized, and she appeared in many movies including *Roman Scandals* (1933), *Stage Door* (1937), and *The Three Musketeers* (1939). While she was acting in a movie called *Dance, Girl, Dance*, she met a band leader from Cuba named Desi Arnaz. They fell in love and got married in 1940.

From 1948-1951, Mrs. Arnaz starred in a radio show called *My Favorite Husband*. In 1950, Mr. and Mrs. Arnaz founded Desilu Productions (notice how parts of "Desi" and "Lucille" were included in the name). CBS Productions agreed to help them produce a television show called *I Love Lucy*, which first aired on television on October 15, 1951.

In *I Love Lucy*, Mrs. Arnaz got to show the world her talent as a comedian. She played a character named Lucy Ricardo, and Mr. Arnaz played her husband, Ricky. William Frawley and Vivian Vance played the parts of their neighbors and good friends, Fred and Ethel Mertz. The show included 180 episodes and ran for six years until 1957.

It was one of the top-rated television shows in America. More people watched the 1953 episode in which Little Ricky was born than U.S. President Dwight D. Eisenhower's first inauguration.

Sadly, in 1960, Mr. and Mrs. Arnaz divorced. In 1962, Mrs. Arnaz became the sole owner of Desilu Productions, and this made her the first woman to ever own a television company. She continued to act in movies and starred in three more television shows: *The Lucy Show* (1962-1968), *Here's Lucy* (1968-1973), and *Life with Lucy* (1986).

Lucille Ball was one of the most famous and influential actresses of all time, and her work inspired other famous comedians. In addition, Desilu Productions went on to make more famous TV shows, such as *The Dick Van Dyke Show*, *Star Trek*, and *Mission: Impossible*.

The *I Love Lucy* foursome: back: William Frawley and Desi Arnaz; front: Vivian Vance and Lucille Ball

Vivian Vance and Lucille Ball acting in the I Love Lucy episode "Job Switching"

FUN FACT

Lucille Ball was well known for her dyed red hair that she had while on the *I Love Lucy* show. In real life, though, her hair was brown.

Jesse Owens
1913 – 1980

Jesse Owens

Born: September 12, 1913, in Oakville, Alabama

Died: March 31, 1980, in Tucson, Arizona

Wife: Minnie Solomon (married 1935–1980)

Children: Gloria, Marlene, Beverly

As a young boy, James Cleveland Owens (who was later called Jesse) loved to run track and was one of the fastest kids in his neighborhood in Oakville, Alabama. When he was nine years old, his family moved to Ohio, and he became more interested in running. Jesse's track coach, Charles Riley, helped and encouraged him in his efforts to improve at the sport.

In 1933, Jesse competed in three track and field competitions at the National Interscholastic Championship in Chicago, Illinois. He tied the world record for the fastest 100-yard dash at 9.4 seconds. In that same year, he began attending Ohio State University (still famous today for graduating very good athletes), and he continued to train, win championships, and set many track records.

In 1936, Mr. Owens represented the United States at the Summer Olympics in Berlin, Germany. At this time in history, it was extremely controversial for a black person to be participating in the games. He was looked down upon by people like Adolf Hitler, the German chancellor who believed that white people were superior to black people. Mr. Owens shocked everyone at the Olympics that year when he won four gold medals in track and field for the 100 meter sprint, 200 meter sprint, 4x100 meter relay, and the long jump. This was one of the greatest Olympic accomplishments of all time, and it made Mr. Owens famous all around the world.

Mr. Owens did not have any major athletic accomplishments after the Olympics, and life was tough financially for him for a while. He even worked as a playground janitor. However, in 1955, because of his great accomplishments earlier in life, he was appointed by the U.S. government to be a goodwill ambassador. As an ambassador, throughout the 1950s, 60s, and 70s, he traveled around the world, speaking out for certain causes and helped to strengthen friendships between the United States and other countries. In 1976, he was awarded the Presidential Medal of Freedom from U.S. President Gerald Ford.

Jesse Owens was one of the most famous athletes in history, and his life story has inspired many people around the world.

Jesse Owens at the 1936 Olympics in Berlin, Germany

Jesse Owens speaking in 1976 in the East Garden at the White House after receiving the Presidential Medal of Freedom from President Ford

FUN FACT

In 2016, a movie called *Race*, directed by Stephen Hopkins, was released, and it was based on Jesse Owens's early life.

John F. Kennedy
1917 - 1963

John F. Kennedy

Born: May 29, 1917, in Brookline, Massachusetts

Died: November 22, 1963, in Dallas, Texas

Wife: Jacqueline Onassis (married 1953-1963)

Children: Arabella, Caroline, John Jr., and Patrick

John Fitzgerald Kennedy (JFK) grew up in Brookline, Massachusetts, and he had eight brothers and sisters. Throughout his childhood, John suffered from occasional poor health, partly as a result of having had scarlet fever, which was very serious in those days. Even after recovering, he suffered from mysterious illnesses for much of his childhood and adult life.

After attending public school and some private schools growing up, John went on to attend Princeton University in 1935 for two months, but he had to leave because of his poor health. He later attended and graduated from Harvard University, where he studied politics.

When America entered World War II in 1941, John joined the United States Navy. One time during the war, while he was the commander of a boat called PT-109, the Japanese destroyed his ship by smashing into it with a huge warship. Although some of the men on board died, John helped save some of the surviving crew. This made him a war hero, and as a result, he received two awards: the Purple Heart and the Marine Corps Medal.

In 1946, Mr. Kennedy began his political career when he was elected into the U.S. House of Representatives. He worked there for seven years and was later elected into the U.S. Senate in 1953.

In 1960, Mr. Kennedy ran for president as a Democrat against Republican Richard Nixon, and he won the election by a very small margin. During Mr. Kennedy's presidency, America and Russia were involved in a "Space Race" to see who could accomplish things in space first. President Kennedy worked hard to encourage and motivate NASA to put an astronaut on the moon before 1970. The United States succeeded and won the Space Race in 1969 when

Neil Armstrong, an American astronaut, became the first person to walk on the moon.

During this same time, America was dealing with many problems with a country called Cuba. America tried several times to help the Cubans get rid of their communist leader, Fidel Castro, but their plans failed. The Soviet Union, another communist nation, began sending missiles to Cuba. Since Cuba is located so closely to the United States, people were worried that they would shoot the missiles at America. President Kennedy made an agreement with Russian leader Nikita Khrushchev to remove the missiles from Cuba. This whole event is known as the "Cuban Missile Crisis."

President Kennedy also worked to end segregation in America, which was when black people were treated unfairly compared to white people. At this same time, Martin Luther King Jr. was an influential civil rights leader in America.

Near the end of 1963, President Kennedy started to campaign for his second term as president. While campaigning in Dallas, Texas, President Kennedy was riding in a motorcade (a series of cars moving slowly, carrying someone important) with his wife, Jacqueline, and the governor of Texas and his wife. During the parade, a man named Lee Harvey Oswald shot President Kennedy. The driver of the president's car rushed to the hospital, but sadly, President Kennedy died shortly after on November 22, 1963. After his death, Vice President Lyndon B. Johnson became America's next president.

John F. Kennedy was one of the most famous and popular United States presidents and world leaders of all time.

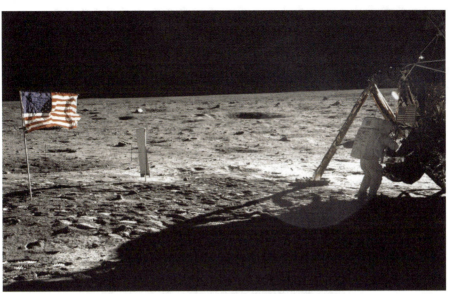

Neil Armstrong on the moon in 1969 next to the Eagle spacecraft (When the spacecraft landed, Mr. Armstrong famously said, "The Eagle has landed.")

FUN FACT

At the age of forty-three, John F. Kennedy was the youngest person to be elected president. He was also the only U.S. president to practice the Roman Catholic religion.

Nelson Mandela
1918 – 2013

Nelson Mandela

Born: July 18, 1918, in Mvezo, South Africa

Died: December 5, 2013, in Johannesburg, South Africa

Wives: Evelyn Mase (married 1944–1958), Winnie Madikizela (married 1958–1996), Graça Machel (married 1998–2013)

Children: Madiba, Makaziwe, Makgatho, Pumla, Zenani, Zindzi

Rolihlahla was a member of Thimbu royalty in South Africa, and his father, Gadla Henry Mphakanyiswa, was the chief of the village of Mvezo. Rolihlahla was given the English name Nelson by his first teacher in school, and it stuck with him for the rest of his life.

In 1939, Nelson enrolled at the University of Fort Hare and also later attended the University of Witwatersrand from 1943-1949 (both in South Africa). While attending these universities, Nelson became more aware of how non-white people were mistreated and segregated in South Africa.

In 1943, he joined and became an active member in the African National Congress (ANC). As part of his work with the ANC, Nelson created the "Spear of the Nation," which was a group of soldiers who would fight for the ANC. In 1961, he was arrested for allegedly planning to bomb government buildings as a way of protesting the South African government but was eventually acquitted (found to be innocent). However, one year later, in 1962, he was arrested again for illegally leaving the country and was sentenced to five years in prison. In 1964, Mr. Mandela was put on trial again for attempting to overthrow the government. He was found guilty and was sentenced to life in prison.

While in prison, Mr. Mandela became famous around the world as more and more people heard about his efforts to try to end segregation against non-whites in South Africa. This policy of discrimination was called apartheid. President Frederik Willem de Klerk of South Africa wanted to end apartheid, and on February 11, 1990, he released Mr.

Mandela from prison. In 1993, the two men won the Nobel Peace Prize together.

In 1994, apartheid was abolished. That same year, Mr. Mandela was elected president of South Africa and served until 1999. After his presidency ended, he continued to support various causes, including the fight against the AIDs disease, which sadly, killed his son Makgatho.

Nelson Mandela was one of the most famous civil rights leaders in history.

Nelson Mandela's cell in Robben Island Prison, South Africa

Nelson Mandela with his second wife, Winnie, on the day he was released from prison

Nelson Mandela voting in the 1994 South African elections

Nelson Mandela receiving the Nobel Peace Prize in 1993

INTERESTING FACT

In 1992, Nelson Mandela played the part of a teacher in a movie called *Malcolm X*. Malcolm X was an American Muslim minister and civil rights leader in America during the mid-20th century. He encouraged the use of violence in civil rights protests.

Pope John Paul II
1920 - 2005

Pope John Paul II

Born: May 18, 1920, in Wadowice, Poland

Died: April 2, 2005, in the Apostolic Palace, Vatican City (a small, independent city-state in Italy that is the headquarters of the Roman Catholic Church; it is the smallest country in the world)

Wife: None

Children: None

During World War II, the Nazis were occupying Poland, and Karol Wojtyla wanted to become a priest in the Roman Catholic Church. However, he had to attend a secret seminary (a place that trains priests/ministers) in Krakow, Poland, so that the Nazis, who hated Catholics, would not find out.

In 1946, after the war ended, Karol was ordained as a Catholic priest. He then went to Rome, Italy, where he completed his Doctorate degree in Catholic theology. In 1948, he returned to Poland and served in several different parishes in and around the city of Krakow. Parishes are small areas of land that have their own Catholic church and priest assigned to them. Karol was smart and had a kind personality, and he inspired a lot of his young students.

In 1958, he became the bishop of Ombi in Poland. A few years later, he participated in the Second Vatican Council, which lasted from 1962-1965, and he helped to make important decisions about the Catholic Church's position in the world. In 1964, Karol became the Archbishop of Krakow, and in 1967, Pope Paul VI made him a cardinal.

On October 16, 1978, Cardinal Karol Wojtyla was elected pope, which is the highest position in the Roman Catholic Church, and he changed his name to John Paul. He was the first pope from Poland and the first pope who was not from Italy in over 400 years. Sadly, in 1981, Pope John Paul II was shot by a Turkish man named Mehmet Ali Agca. Thankfully, he recovered and later visited Mr. Agca in prison to forgive him for what he had done to him.

During his time as pope, Pope John Paul II visited over 100 countries, fought for human rights, and spoke out against things like abortion, gay marriage, and capital punishment. He also made apologies for bad things the Catholic Church had done in the past and worked to improve the relationships between Catholicism and other religions, particularly Judaism, the religion of the Jews.

Pope John Paul II also played a big role in ending communism in Poland, his home country, and the rest of Eastern Europe. Communism ended there with the tearing down of the Berlin Wall in 1989. He had very good relationships with people like Soviet Union leader Mikhail Gorbachev, Mother Teresa, South African President Nelson Mandela, and United States President Ronald Reagan.

In 2005, Pope John Paul II died of Parkinson's disease, which negatively affects a person's nervous system and causes the body to tremble. He was one of the most beloved popes and world leaders of all time. In 2014, he was canonized (made a saint) by the Roman Catholic Church.

Pope John Paul II in Yankee Stadium in 1979

Pope John Paul II holding a Koala bear in Brisbane, Australia, in 1986

President Ronald Reagan and Pope John Paul II in Alaska in 1984

FUN FACT

There are over 2,000 bishops in the Roman Catholic Church around the world. During his reign, Pope John Paul II knew each of the bishops' names by heart. He was also seen by more people than anyone else in history. It is estimated that over 500 million people saw him during his lifelong travels of over 750,000 miles.

Fidel Castro
1926 - 2016

Fidel Castro

Born: August 13, 1926, in Birán, Cuba

Died: November 25, 2016, in Havana, Cuba

Wives: Mirta Díaz-Balart (married 1948-1955), Dalia Soto del Valle (married 1980-2016)

Children: Fidel (also known as "Fidelito"), Antonio, Alejandro, Alexis, Alexander (known as "Alex"), Ángel, Alina, Jorge, Francisca (Alina was born to a woman named Natalia Clews, and Jorge and Francisca were born to women whose names are unknown.)

From 1945-1950, Fidel Castro studied law at the University of Havana in Cuba. It was there that he began to protest against the government of Cuba because he believed it was corrupt. Castro was originally in favor of a democratic (free) government, and in 1947, he joined the Party of the Cuban People. However, after traveling around Latin America during the late 1940s helping in various revolutions against different governments, he became a socialist.

In 1952, Castro decided to run for a seat in the Cuban House of Representatives, but that same year, Fulgencio Batista overthrew the government, cancelled the elections, and became the dictator of Cuba. In 1953, Castro and his younger brother, Raúl, were put in prison for trying to overthrow the government, but they were released two years later. They fled to Mexico, where Castro began plotting a revolution in Cuba. While he was in Mexico, he met a man named Che Guevara, who would become one of his future top leaders in Cuba.

In 1956, Castro returned to Cuba with a small army, but they were defeated by President Fulgencio Batista. They escaped to the hills, and over the next few years, they fought in guerilla warfare against the government. This means that they would carry out surprise attacks (ambushes) in small numbers against government soldiers.

In 1959, after gaining many new supporters in Cuba, Castro finally defeated Batista and his government and became the new leader of Cuba. He declared himself to be a communist and established a communistic government in the country. Communism is a form of government created by Karl Marx and Friedrich Engels. In a communist system, citizens do not own anything because the government controls everything.

Fidel Castro was a harsh dictator, who controlled much of Cuba's economy, industry, and press (newspapers). In 1962, he formed an alliance with the Soviet Union, which led to the Cuban Missile Crisis. He ruled Cuba for almost fifty years and eventually resigned in 2008. His brother, Raúl, became the new leader and ruled for ten years.

Fidel Castro was one of the most infamous communists and dictators in history.

Che Guevara (left) and Fidel Castro (right)

Fidel Castro speaking in Havana, Cuba, in 2006

INTERESTING FACT

Fidel Castro was known for delivering very long speeches. His 1960 speech to the United Nations was the longest on record at four hours and twenty-nine minutes. In 1998, he delivered one of the longest speeches in history in Cuba after he was reelected as president of the country. It was seven and a half hours long.

Martin Luther King Jr.
1929 - 1968

Martin Luther King Jr.

Born: January 25, 1929, in Atlanta, Georgia

Died: April 4, 1968, in Memphis, Tennessee

Wife: Coretta Scott (married 1953-1968)

Children: Yolanda, Martin Luther King III, Dexter, Bernice

Martin Luther King Jr.'s father and grandfather were both ministers, and Martin eventually followed in their footsteps. He attended Morehouse College in Georgia, Crozer Theological Seminary in Pennsylvania, and Boston University in Massachusetts to earn three college degrees. In 1954, he became a minister at Dexter Avenue Baptist Church in Montgomery, Alabama, where he pastored for six years.

While living in Montgomery, Dr. King became involved with civil rights for black people. He was inspired to do something when a black woman named Rosa Parks refused to give up her seat on a bus to a white person. She was arrested for refusing to give up her seat, and Dr. King led black people all over the city in what is known as the Alabama Bus Boycott. A boycott is when a group of people refuse to do something as a way to protest. Many black people stopped using the city's bus system, and so, eventually, bus segregation in Montgomery, Alabama, ended. Segregation is when people are treated unfairly and separated from each other because they have different skin colors. During this time, Dr. King was arrested and imprisoned for his civil rights activities and later released. His house was even bombed by people who hated him.

After the bus boycott, Dr. King continued to fight for equal rights for everyone. During the 1950s, he started the Civil Rights Movement, and in 1957, he helped to found the Southern Christian Leadership Conference. This movement peacefully protested against segregation, and Dr. King gave many important speeches for civil rights. His most famous speech was called the "I Have a Dream" speech, which was given in 1963 during the March on Washington in Washington, D.C.

In 1964, because of Dr. King's hard work, the Civil Rights Act was passed, and it officially ended segregation in America. Dr. King was honored many times for his work, including in 1964, when he became the youngest person to receive the Nobel Peace Prize. However, some people in America were not happy about the new changes for black people. In 1968, an angry white man named James Earl Ray shot and killed Dr. King in Memphis, Tennessee.

Martin Luther King Jr. was one of the most famous and influential civil rights leaders in history. America still honors him today with a national holiday: Martin Luther King Jr. Day on the third Monday in January.

Martin Luther King Jr.'s boyhood home in Atlanta, Georgia

The March on Washington in 1963
(Martin Luther King Jr. is in the center)

FUN FACT

Martin Luther King Jr. received both the Presidential Medal of Freedom in 1977 and the Congressional Gold Medal posthumously (after he died) in 2004. There are also over 730 streets in the United States named after him.

Mikhail Gorbachev
1931 - Present

Mikhail Gorbachev

Born: March 2, 1931, in the village of Privolnoye, present-day Russia

Wife: Raisa Titarenko (married 1953-1999)

Children: Irina

In 1950, Mikhail Gorbachev went to Moscow University and earned a law degree. It was here that he joined the Communist Party and became a very active member. In 1955, he began working as a member of the Communist Youth Organization. Five years later, Mikhail was chosen to represent the city of Stavropol in the Communist Party Congress in Moscow, the capital of the Soviet Union (present-day Russia).

    In 1970, Mr. Gorbachev became the First Secretary for the entire Stavropol area, and one year later, he was selected to be the Secretary of Agriculture for the Communist Party. In 1980, he became a member of the Politburo, which was the most powerful policy-making government authority of the Communist Party in the Soviet Union.

    In 1985, Mr. Gorbachev was elected as the General Secretary of the Communist Party, which made him the leader of the Soviet Union. Unlike many communist leaders before him, Secretary Gorbachev created policies that gave people in the Soviet Union more freedom and rights and also helped to improve the economy. He also worked with U.S. President Ronald Reagan to reach an agreement called the INF Treaty, in which America and the Soviet Union would destroy many of their powerful nuclear weapons/missiles. This agreement helped to end the Cold War between the two countries that had begun in 1945 at the end of World War II and had lasted almost 45 years.

    In 1990, Secretary Gorbachev was awarded the Nobel Peace Prize because of his government policies that created more freedom for the Soviet people and also for his efforts to decrease the number of nuclear weapons in the world.

    Interestingly, in 1991, some of his enemies kidnapped him and said that he was sick and could not rule the country anymore. They wanted to bring back the harsher communist government that had existed before Secretary Gorbachev took office. He was set free a couple days later but resigned as the leader of the Soviet Union on December 25, 1991. His resignation and other issues led to the collapse of the Soviet Union's government just one day later. As a result of the collapse, the independent country of Russia was established, and Boris Yeltsin became its first president, serving from 1991-1999.

Mikhail Gorbachev is one of the most famous world leaders in history and is known around the world for his efforts to help end the Cold War.

President Ronald Reagan and Mikhail Gorbachev signing the INF Treaty on June 1, 1988, at the Grand Kremlin Palace in Moscow, Soviet Union

Mikhail Gorbachev and his granddaughter Anastasia in a Pizza Hut commercial (See "Fun Fact" below)

FUN FACT

In 1997, Mikhail Gorbachev appeared in a Pizza Hut® commercial with his granddaughter, Anastasia. In the commercial, they visit a Pizza Hut® restaurant in Moscow, Russia.

Elvis Presley
1935 - 1977

Elvis Presley

Born: January 8, 1935, in Tupelo, Mississippi

Died: August 16, 1977, at his home, Graceland, in Memphis, Tennessee

Wife: Priscilla Beaulieu (married 1967-1973)

Children: Lisa

Elvis Presley was born an identical twin, but sadly, his twin brother, Jesse, was stillborn (dead at birth). Elvis was raised in a Pentecostal Christian home and grew up going to church and singing there. When he was young, Elvis received a guitar as a present and learned to play it well. This and the influence of church/gospel music were instrumental in him becoming interested in music. The Presley's neighbors would often hear the family singing on their front porch.

In 1954, Elvis went to Sun Record Company in Memphis, Tennessee, and played a couple songs for the people there. Sam Phillips, the head of the record company, really enjoyed his singing. As a result, Elvis began his professional singing career with a song called "That's All Right," and he quickly became very popular on the radio. In 1956, he began to work for RCA Records, and his songs sold over one million copies. One of his most popular songs was called "Heartbreak Hotel" (1956), and it became a number-one hit in the United States.

Elvis Presley was a proficient (active and very accomplished) singer in several different musical genres (categories): Rock 'n' Roll, pop, blues, country, and gospel. Some of his most famous songs from these genres include "Jailhouse Rock," "You Ain't Nothin' but a Hound Dog," "A Mess of Blues," and "Amazing Grace."

During the 1950s and 60s, Elvis became popular all over America, especially with young audiences. Many people came to his stage performances, and he was known as "The King of Rock 'n' Roll." Elvis also acted in over thirty movies, including *Love Me Tender* (1956), *Jailhouse Rock* (1957), and *Change of Habit* (1969). He also made many music videos to go with his songs and appeared on several television shows, including *The Ed Sullivan Show*. In 1973, Elvis gave a concert called *Aloha from Hawaii* over the radio. It was the first concert done by a solo performer that was broadcast around the world, and it helped to make him even more popular.

Elvis Presley was one of the most famous and beloved American singers and actors of all time. He is one of the best-selling solo artists (music performers) in history and has received a place in many different musical halls of fame.

Elvis performing in Tupelo, Mississippi, in 1956

U.S. President Richard Nixon and Elvis Presley in 1970 in the Oval Office of the White House

Graceland, Elvis Presley's home in Memphis, Tennessee

FUN FACT

In 1994, Elvis's daughter, Lisa Marie Presley, married Michael Jackson, who was also a very famous singer.

John Lennon
1940 – 1980

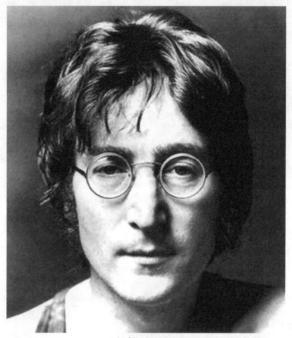

John Lennon

Born: October 9, 1940, in Liverpool, England

Died: December 8, 1980, in New York City, New York

Wives: Cynthia Powell (married 1962–1968), Yoko Ono (married 1969–1980)

Children: John Jr. (known by his middle name Julian), Sean

As a teenager, John Lennon's mother, Julia, taught him how to play the piano and also gave him his first guitar. He spent many hours practicing and playing both instruments.

In 1957, John formed a band called The Quarrymen, and later that same year, he met a young man named Paul McCartney. The two of them began to write and rehearse songs together at Paul's house, and John's first complete song was called "Hello Little Girl." Paul convinced John to let George Harrison, who was only fifteen years old at the time, join their band, which was renamed The Beatles in 1960. John was seen as the leader of the band because he was the oldest.

Later in 1960, The Beatles traveled to Hamburg, Germany, to play at the Indra Club and other places, but the trip was unsuccessful. First, George was deported (forced out of the country) because he was working as a minor below the legal age limit. Then Paul was deported, too, because he was convicted of arson (intentionally setting a fire). John then returned to England after his work permit (permission from the government to work) was taken away.

In 1961, The Beatles performed their first concert in Liverpool, England, and they quickly became very popular. The next year, Ringo Starr joined the band, and they began to record many popular songs, such as "I Want to Hold Your Hand." In 1964, they traveled around the United States, singing in many different concerts. The band was especially popular with young Americans. The Beatles broke up in 1969, and Mr. Lennon began to record songs on his own that were very successful, including "Imagine" (1971), which is one of the most famous songs around the world today.

Sadly, however, in 1980, while he was staying at the Dakota apartment building in New York City, Mr. Lennon was shot and killed by a man named Mark Chapman. Chapman had received Mr. Lennon's autograph on an album just several hours earlier and had been waiting to kill him when he returned to his hotel. He claims to have done it so that he could become famous (infamous).

John Lennon was one of the most famous and popular singers of all time, and The Beatles are considered by many people to be the greatest band in history.

John Lennon recording his song "Imagine"

The Beatles arriving in New York City in 1964
(From left to right: John Lennon, Paul McCartney, George Harrison, and Ringo Starr)

FUN FACT

When John Lennon received his first guitar, his aunt Mimi said to him, "The guitar's all very well, John, but you'll never make a living at it."

Muhammad Ali
1942 - 2016

Muhammad Ali

Born: January 17, 1942, in Louisville, Kentucky

Died: June 3, 2016, in Scottsdale, Arizona

Wives: Sonji Roi (married 1964-1966), Belinda Boyd (married 1967-1976), Veronica Porsche (married 1977-1986), Yolanda "Lonnie" Williams (married 1986-2016)

Children: Maryum, Rasheda, Jamillah, Muhammad Ali, Jr., Miya, Khaliah, Hana, Laila, Asaad (adopted) (Miya was born to a woman named Patricia Harvell, and Khaliah was born to a woman named Wanda Bolton.)

When he was twelve years old, Cassius Clay, Jr. learned how to box from a policeman who taught him self-defense. Cassius soon discovered that he had a natural talent for the sport and went on to win 100 amateur (non-professional) boxing matches.

In 1960, Cassius represented the United States of America at the Olympic Games in Rome, Italy, and won a Gold Medal in boxing. When he returned home to America, he became a professional boxer, which means that he was paid to play the sport. He was a great boxer and defeated many of his opponents.

In 1964, Cassius converted to Islam (became a Muslim) and changed his name to Muhammad Ali, in honor of Islam's founder, Muhammad.

At this time in history, a man named Sonny Liston was the heavyweight boxing champion of the world. Mr. Ali won tournament after tournament, and eventually, in 1964, he fought against Mr. Liston for the world title. It was a tough fight, but Mr. Ali defeated him because Mr. Liston refused to enter the ring for the seventh and final round. Mr. Ali was crowned the heavyweight boxing champion of the world.

Throughout the 1970s, Mr. Ali was involved in more famous boxing matches, including his 1974 victory in the fight "Rumble in the Jungle" against George Foreman. Because of this match, Mr. Ali won the title of Undisputed Heavyweight Champion of the world.

In 1981, Mr. Ali retired from boxing and devoted much of his time to supporting charities. He also struggled for many years with Parkinson's disease, which negatively affects a person's nervous system and causes the body to tremble.

In 2005, he was awarded the Presidential Medal of Freedom from United States President George W. Bush. It is America's highest civilian honor and was awarded to Mr. Ali for his devotion to humanitarian efforts, world peace, civil rights, and religious liberty.

Muhammad Ali is known by many people around the world as the greatest boxer of all time and also as a defender of human rights. In 2001, a film called *Ali*, directed by Michael Mann, was made about his life, and a documentary called *I Am Ali*, directed by Clare Lewins, was released in 2014.

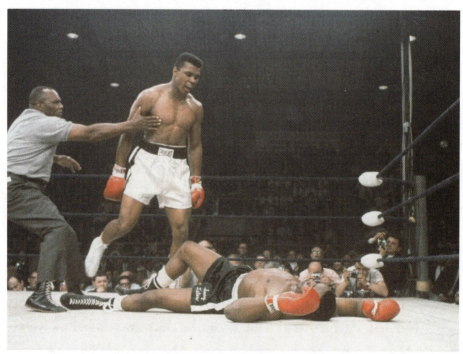

Muhammad Ali taunting Sonny Liston in 1964

President George W. Bush awarding Muhammad Ali the Presidential Medal of Freedom in 2005

FUN FACT

Before entering the boxing ring to fight Sonny Liston, Muhammad Ali said something for which he became very famous: "I float like a butterfly and sting like a bee." This line was imitated by the writers of the 2006 Disney Pixar film *Cars* when Lightning McQueen says, "I float like a Cadillac and sting like a Beemer."

Donald J. Trump
1946 – Present

Donald J. Trump

Born: June 14, 1946, in New York City, New York

Wives: Ivana Zelnickova (married 1977-1992), Marla Maples (married 1993-1999), and Melania Knauss (married 2005-present)

Children: Donald Jr., Ivanka, Eric, Tiffany, Barron

In 1968, Donald John Trump entered the Wharton School of the University of Pennsylvania and studied economics. While in college, Donald worked for his father, Fred, at the Trump Management Company. In 1971, he took over his father's business and renamed it The Trump Organization. This was the beginning of Mr. Trump's career as a businessman.

In 1973, Mr. Trump began to build many apartments and other buildings called condominiums or condos. He has been constructing buildings in America and other parts of the world ever since, including one in New York City called Trump Tower. In addition to buildings, Mr. Trump has also built golf courses and casinos. Since becoming a successful businessman, he has acted in movies and even had his own television show called *The Apprentice*, which ran from 2004-2017.

Since he owns so many buildings and properties, Mr. Trump has become one of the richest people in America. In 2015, he released papers saying that he was worth over eight billion dollars.

In addition to business, Mr. Trump was also interested in politics for many years before being elected as the president of the United States. He considered running for governor of New York and president several times. In 2000, he decided to run for president under the Reform Party ticket, but he dropped out of the race at the beginning of the primaries. Mr. Trump ran for president again in 2016 as a Republican and defeated Hillary Clinton, a Democrat and wife of former President Bill Clinton.

During his campaign, Mr. Trump's slogan was "Make America Great Again." He promised to do many things as president, such as improving the U.S. economy by restoring

American jobs, rebuilding the military, and building a border wall between the United States and Mexico to stop illegal immigrants from entering the United States.

Donald Trump is the oldest (age 70) and richest person to have ever been elected president of the United States. On June 12, 2018, he met with North Korean leader Kim Jong-un for the DPRK-USA Singapore Summit in Sentosa, Singapore. It was an historic event because it was the first meeting ever between the leaders of the United States and North Korea.

President Donald Trump is one of the most famous leaders in the world today.

Trump International Hotel in Washington, D.C., United States

President Donald Trump and North Korean leader Kim Jong-un on June 12, 2018, for the DPRK-USA Singapore Summit

FUN FACT

Donald Trump has his own plane called a Boeing 757. While he was campaigning for president, people called his plane "Trump Force One" because the American president's plane is called "Air Force One."

George W. Bush
1946 – Present

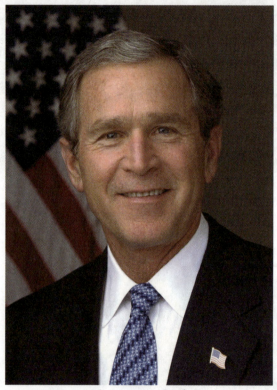

George W. Bush

Born: July 6, 1946, in New Haven, Connecticut

Wife: Laura Welch (married 1977–present)

Children: Barbara, Jenna

George Walker Bush's father, George H.W. Bush, was the forty-first president of the United States. When George W. Bush was elected president, this made him and his father the second father and son to each become president. The first pair was John Adams and his son, John Quincy Adams, the second and sixth presidents of the United States.

George's family moved to Texas when he was young. He loved to play sports in school and wanted to become a professional baseball player. However, he decided to attend Yale University instead, just like his father had.

In 1968, George graduated from Yale University and joined the Texas Air National Guard. He learned how to fly planes, such as the F-102. In 1974, after completing his time in the National Guard, George returned home to Texas and became part-owner of a baseball team called the Texas Rangers.

In 1988, when his father, George H.W. Bush, ran for president, Mr. Bush helped him by organizing his campaign. A few years later, in 1994, he decided to run for governor of Texas, and he won.

In 2000, George W. Bush ran for president as a Republican against Al Gore. Mr. Gore had been President Bill Clinton's vice president. The election was very close, and the votes from the state of Florida had to be recounted. After the votes were tallied, George W. Bush was declared the winner of the election by a small margin.

As soon as he took office, President Bush worked to lower taxes. In fact, in 2002, he signed a bill that lowered taxes more than any other previous president before him.

In addition to the many stresses and challenges of being president, President Bush had to deal with what would turn out to be one of the saddest days in American history. On September 11, 2001, a group of Islamic terrorists hijacked (took control of) four American airplanes. The terrorists crashed two of the planes into the Twin Towers in New York City. More terrorists then crashed a third plane into a building in Washington, D.C., called the Pentagon. Even more terrorists had taken over a fourth plane, but some very brave people on the plane tried to stop them. The plane ended up crashing into a field in Pennsylvania, and everyone on board died. Almost 3,000 people died that day and more than 6,000 were injured.

After these tragic attacks, President Bush gave an important speech at the crash site in New York City (called "Ground Zero") to try to comfort the American people. He also sent American soldiers to a country called Iraq to stop more Islamic terrorists from attacking the United States again. He also did this to try to stop the terrorists from hurting and killing people in the Middle East. This started the Iraq War, which lasted from 2003-2011.

Since his presidency ended in 2009, George W. Bush has worked to support different charities and has written a couple books, including *Decision Points* (2010). He also took up painting as a hobby, and his works are featured in a book called *Portraits of Courage*. President Bush is one of the most famous American presidents and world leaders in history.

President George W. Bush (holding the megaphone) speaking at "Ground Zero" after the September 11, 2001, attacks

FUN FACT

George W. Bush loves baseball and owns 250 baseballs that have been signed by famous players.

Steve Jobs
1955 – 2011

Steve Jobs

Born: February 24, 1955, in San Francisco, California

Died: October 5, 2011, in Palo Alto, California

Wife: Laurene Powell (married 1991–2011)

Children: Lisa, Reed, Erin, Eve (Lisa was born to a woman named Chrisann Brennan before Mr. Jobs was married.)

As a young boy, Steve Jobs loved to work on electronics with his adoptive father, Paul. Together, they would take things apart and put them back together again. As he grew up, Steve continued to have an interest in electronics. When he was thirteen years old, he met a young man named Steve Wozniak, who shared his interests.

After attending Reed College in Oregon, Steve (Jobs) went to work for a computer company called Atari. He began to spend more time with Steve Wozniak, who designed and built his own personal computer. In 1976, together with Ronald Wayne, the two men founded the Apple Computer Company, and the first computer they released was called Apple I, designed by Mr. Wozniak.

The Apple Computer Company began to grow, and they continued to design and release new versions of computers. In 1984, Mr. Jobs introduced the Macintosh (MAC) computer. However, one year later, in 1985, he resigned from Apple because his new computer was not doing as well as the PC model from the company IBM, and Apple was actually losing money. Soon after that, he founded a new company called NeXT Computer, but it was unsuccessful.

Then, in 1986, Mr. Jobs bought a graphics company (later called Pixar) that went on to make many successful animated motion pictures for Walt Disney Studios, including *Toy Story*, *Finding Nemo*, and *A Bug's Life*. Mr. Jobs earned a lot of money from this company, and in 1997, he returned to Apple, became the CEO (Chief Executive Officer), and began to develop many more revolutionary (new, important, and extraordinary) products.

Between 2001-2010, the iPod, iTunes music software, iPhone, and iPad were all released. Hundreds of millions of them have sold since then (or, in iTunes's case, been downloaded) around the world, and Apple has become one of the most successful American companies in history. Steve Jobs was one of the greatest inventors and innovators (idea person) of all time.

Steve Wozniak

Apple I, the first computer released by the Apple Computer Company

Steve Jobs unveiling the iPad in 2010 in San Francisco, California

FUN FACT

The Disney Pixar movie *Brave* was released in 2012, one year after Steve Jobs died of cancer. The film was dedicated to him in honor of his important position as the original owner of Pixar Studios.

Bill Gates
1955 - Present

Bill Gates

Born: October 28, 1955, in Seattle, Washington

Wife: Melinda French (married 1994-present)

Children: Jennifer, Rory, Phoebe

William (Known as Bill) Gates was first introduced to computers as a teenager at Lakeside Preparatory School in Washington State. It was here that he met Paul Allen, who became his business partner later in life. At this time in history, computers were very large and took up a lot of space. The desktop computer was not invented until 1975 by Pier Perotto. Bill's first computer program was a version of the game Tic-Tac-Toe. He also worked with a company called Computer Center Corporation to learn more about computers. At the same time, he started a business with Paul Allen designing computer programs to help with the traffic system in Seattle, Washington.

In 1973, Bill attended Harvard University to study law. In 1974, he designed a software program called BASIC with Paul Allen for Alistair, a computer company. In 1975, Bill dropped out of Harvard University and founded his own computer software company called Microsoft.

Mr. Gates's company began to do very well, and he sold its operating system to many important companies, including IBM (International Business Machines) in 1980. In 1983, Microsoft Word (the program used to type this book) was launched. In 1985, the Microsoft Windows operating system was released and was eventually proven to be better than Apple's operating system. (Apple is another big computer company.) In 1995, Windows 95, an updated operating system, was released, and it was an important new development in software operating systems.

Microsoft has continued to grow and release new programs, and since 1995, Mr. Gates has been listed as the richest person in the world several times. He is currently worth over 90 billion dollars. His home in Washington State took seven years to build and is worth over 127 million dollars. It has seven bedrooms, twenty-four bathrooms, a twenty-three car garage, a large swimming pool, a movie theater that seats twenty people, and a gym. Guests enter the house through a private tunnel. In addition, Mr. Gates owns several vehicles, four private jets, a helicopter, and a seaplane.

    Bill Gates is one of the most famous, successful, and influential entrepreneurs (someone who organizes and runs a business) in history. His Microsoft programs are used all around the world today.

1975 Microsoft logo

Steve Jobs and Bill Gates in 2007 at the D5 Conference in San Diego, California

Bill Gates's home in Washington State

FUN FACT

In 2000, Bill Gates and his wife founded the Bill and Melinda Gates Foundation, and they have given almost 30 billion dollars to charity since then.

Michael Jackson
1958 – 2009

Michael Jackson

Born: August 29, 1958, in Gary, Indiana

Died: June 25, 2009, at his home in Los Angeles, California

Wives: Lisa Presley (married 1994-1996), Debbie Rowe (married 1996-1999)

Children: Michael Joseph Jackson Jr. (nicknamed "Prince"), Paris, Prince Michael Jackson II (nicknamed "Blanket")

While growing up in Gary, Indiana, Michael Jackson's mother, Katherine, taught him and his four brothers how to sing folk and gospel music. In the early 1960s, Michael and four of his brothers started a band called The Jackson 5. They became very popular doing shows and talent contests in the Midwest region of the United States. The brothers were (in birth order): Jackie, Tito, Jermaine, Marlon, and Michael.

The Jackson 5 started off performing at talent shows and clubs, and in 1967, they signed a contract with Steeltown Records and released two songs. In 1968, The Jackson 5 left Steeltown Records and signed a contract with Motown Records. They became very popular and sold millions of copies of their songs, including "ABC," "I Want You Back," and several others.

In 1971, Berry Gordy, the head of Motown Records, began to release albums of just Michael singing, and they began to sell as much as The Jackson 5 albums. Between 1972-1975, Michael released four albums, including *Got To Be There* (1972), and *Music & Me* (1973). During this time, he was a popular American teenage icon, which means he was very famous and recognizable, especially among young people. In 1978, Michael also acted as the scarecrow in a movie called *The Wiz*, which helped him to become even more well-known.

In 1982, Mr. Jackson released an album called *Thriller* with the help of a record producer named Quincy Jones. Some songs on this album include "Beat It" and "Billie Jean." The album has sold over forty million copies, and it helped to make Michael Jackson the most popular singer of the 1980s. Today it is one of the best-selling albums of all time. In 1991, Mr. Jackson released the album *Dangerous*, which included one of his most popular songs, called "Black or White." In all, he released ten albums during his lifetime. He also made many music videos to go with his songs, performed in many concerts all around the world, and founded several charity organizations.

In addition to his work for different record companies, Michael Jackson also worked for PepsiCo, a soda pop company, and he performed in some of their commercials. Interestingly, in 1984, while filming a Pepsi commercial, his hair caught on fire when he stepped too close to a fireworks explosion behind him. He had to be rushed to the hospital, but thankfully, he recovered.

Michael Jackson was one of the most popular and famous American singers of all time. He is known as the "King of Pop."

The Jackson 5 performing on their first television special in 1969
(From left to right: Tito, Marlon, Michael, Jackie, and Jermaine)

Michael Jackson performing his song "Jam" in 1992 while on his Dangerous World Tour in Europe

Michael Jackson's Neverland Ranch in Los Olivos, California

FUN FACT

Michael Jackson owned a ranch called Neverland Ranch in Los Olivos, California. At this ranch, he had two pet llamas named Louis and Lola.

Princess Diana
1961 – 1997

Princess Diana

Born: July 1, 1961, in Sandringham, Norfolk, England

Died: August 31, 1997, in Paris, France

Husband: Charles, Prince of Wales (married 1981-1996)

Children: William, Henry (known as Harry)

Diana Spencer had royal ancestors through her father's family line. Her father, John Spencer, was a descendant of King Charles II of England, and her mother, Frances Kydd, was the daughter of an Anglo-Irish baron. Diana also grew up knowing Prince Andrew and Prince Edward, two of Queen Elizabeth II's sons.

In 1977, Prince Andrew and Prince Edward's older brother, Charles, met Diana for the first time, and they began to get to know each other. In 1980, they started to take walks and go fishing together. Eventually, they decided to get married. Their wedding took place on July 29, 1981, in St. Paul's Cathedral in London, England. Hundreds of millions of people around the world watched the historic wedding on television. It was called the "wedding of the century," and it was significant because Diana was the first British citizen to marry royalty since the 1600s.

Throughout the rest of her life, Princess Diana spoke out for and supported many different causes, including trying to find a cure for the AIDS disease and leprosy. She became very popular and traveled all over the world. She was beloved by the English people because she believed that British royalty should have regular contact with the people.

Princess Diana also spent time in homeless shelters in London and visited many hospital patients who had HIV and AIDS. She also met and got to know many famous people, including United States President Ronald Reagan, Mother Teresa, and Michael Jackson.

Sadly, Princess Diana and Prince Charles divorced on August 28, 1996. Just one year later, Princess Diana died in a car accident with Dodi Fayed. Over two billion people watched her funeral around the world, and she is still beloved and admired today as one of England's greatest princesses. She is known as the "People's Princess."

Princess Diana's 25-foot-long wedding dress train

Princess Diana and Prince Charles on their wedding day

Mother Teresa and Princess Diana in New York City, New York

Princess Diana dancing with President Ronald Reagan at the White House

FUN FACT

Princess Diana's silk wedding dress had 10,000 pearls sewn onto it, and her train (long, flowing back portion of a wedding dress) was 25 feet long! The dress cost around $115,000.

Barack Obama
1961 - Present

Barack Obama

Born: August 4, 1961, in Honolulu, Hawaii

Wife: Michelle Robinson (married 1992-present)

Children: Malia, Sasha

Barack Obama's mother, Ann, was from America and his father, Barack Sr., was from Kenya, Africa. Barack's parents divorced in 1964 when he was young. One year later, Barack's mother married a man named Lolo Soetoro from Indonesia. Barack and his mother moved to Indonesia and lived there for a few years. Eventually, in 1971, he returned to Hawaii to live with his grandparents, and he attended school at Punahou Academy.

After completing high school, Barack attended a few different colleges, including Occidental College in California, Columbia College in New York, and Harvard Law School. At Columbia College, Barack studied government and politics, and at Harvard, he studied law.

In 1992, Mr. Obama began to teach about United States constitutional law at the University of Chicago in Illinois. In 1996, Mr. Obama began his political career when he was elected as an Illinois state senator. Mr. Obama worked as a state senator until 2004 when he was elected as a United States Senator.

In 2008, Mr. Obama ran for president as a Democrat and defeated Republican candidate John McCain. This is significant in American history because Mr. Obama is the first black man to be elected president.

During Mr. Obama's presidency, many terrorists did awful things in America and the Middle East. In one instance, a terrorist attacked the Fort Hood military base in Texas. America then suffered a similar attack in 2012 at the U.S. Consulate in Benghazi, Libya, when Islamic terrorists killed four Americans. Thankfully, during President Obama's second term, the U.S. Navy SEAL

Team Six was successful in killing an Islamic terrorist leader named Osama bin Laden. He was the leader behind the terrorist attacks on America on September 11, 2001.

Also, during his presidency, Mr. Obama signed a law called the Affordable Care Act, which created a healthcare program known as "Obamacare."

Barack Obama is one of the most famous American presidents and world leaders today.

Barack Obama taking the Presidential Oath of Office in 2009

President Barack Obama campaigning in Iowa in 2012

Actors in the 2012 television film
SEAL Team Six: The Raid on Osama Bin Laden

FUN FACT

As a teenager, Barack Obama worked at an ice cream shop called Baskin-Robbins.

Michael Jordan
1963 – Present

Michael Jordan

Born: February 17, 1963, in Brooklyn, New York

Wives: Juanita Vanoy (married 1989-2006), Yvette Prieto (married 2013-present)

Children: Jeffrey, Marcus, Jasmine, Victoria, Ysabel

Michael Jordan began to develop and increase his basketball skills while at Emsley A. Laney High School in Wilmington, North Carolina. While he was there, he played in the 1981 McDonald's All-American Basketball game, in which he scored the most points. This was the first time he was able to really show his basketball skills that he had worked hard at developing in high school.

From 1982-1984, Michael attended the University of North Carolina at Chapel Hill and studied cultural geography. During his time there, he became a player for the NCAA (National Collegiate Athletic Association), and in 1982, he scored the winning point in the NCAA championship game for his school's team against Georgetown University. Mr. Jordan has described this event as a turning point in his basketball career.

In 1984, he played for the United States Olympic Basketball team in Los Angeles, California, and helped the U.S. win a gold medal. That same year, Mr. Jordan was drafted to play for the Chicago Bulls NBA (National Basketball Association) team, and he left college.

Over the next few years, he scored thousands of points for his team, set new records, and was in his first NBA All-Star Game in 1985. During the 1990s, Mr. Jordan helped the Chicago Bulls win six NBA championships. He was especially famous for the way he could "fly" through the air from the foul line to slam dunk the basketball. When he would do this move, he almost always had his mouth wide open with his tongue sticking out. Because of his great physical ability to jump like this, he was given the nickname "Air Jordan."

In 1992, he went to the Olympics in Barcelona, Spain, and again helped the U.S. team win a gold medal. The U.S. Olympic basketball team that year was called the "Dream Team" and included other famous basketball players like Larry Bird from the Boston Celtics and "Magic" Johnson from the LA Lakers. ("Magic" Johnson was my mother's favorite NBA player, and she actually got to meet him while she and my dad were in Los Angeles one time.)

In 1992, Michael Jordan decided to retire from basketball to play professional baseball. However, he was not very successful at it and returned to play basketball for the Chicago Bulls in 1995.

In 1999, he retired again, and in 2000, he became part owner of the Washington Wizards basketball team. In 2001, however, he decided to join the team as one of its players. In 2003, he retired from the game for the last time, and in 2006, he became part owner of the Charlotte Hornets basketball team. In addition to being a team owner, Michael Jordan enjoys playing golf, is very involved in charity work, and has a line of Nike® shoes called Air Jordan®.

Michael Jordan is considered by many people to be the greatest basketball player of all time.

Michael Jordan "flying" through the air to dunk a basketball

Air Jordan® shoes

Michael Jordan playing baseball

FUN FACT

Michael Jordan acted in a 1996 science fiction movie called *Space Jam*, directed by Joe Pytka. He played opposite *Looney Tunes* cartoon characters like Bugs Bunny because the film mixed cartoon animation with live-action footage. Mr. Jordan was paid 20 million dollars to appear in the film.

J.K. Rowling
1965 - Present

J.K. Rowling

Born: July 31, 1965, in Yate, Gloucestershire, England

Husbands: Jorge Arantes (married 1992-1993), Dr. Neil Murray (married 2001-present)

Children: Jessica, David, Mackenzie

As a young girl in England, Joanne Rowling loved to make up stories and write books, including one about a rabbit, called "Rabbit." She later studied French and Classics at Exeter University in Devon, England. One day, in 1990, she was sitting on a train when she thought up the idea for *Harry Potter*, which eventually became a seven-book fantasy series about a young boy named Harry, who is training to be a wizard. For the next several years, Joanne spent much of her time writing the first book. She was influenced by personal experiences and also by great works of literature, such as *The Lord of the Rings* by J.R.R. Tolkien.

While she was writing the *Harry Potter* books, Ms. Rowling experienced personal tragedy when, in 1990, her mother, Anne, died, and three years later, she and her first husband, Jorge, got divorced. She also lived in poverty (poor and difficult conditions) for several years. Some people believe that Ms. Rowling's depression at this time caused her to create the Dementors, which are evil characters in her *Harry Potter* books.

In 1997, *Harry Potter and the Philosopher's Stone* was published by Bloomsbury Children's Books. Ms. Rowling's publishers wanted her to have two initials instead of using her first name because they thought that some young boys might not read the book if they knew that it was written by a woman. So, she gave herself the middle name Kathleen, which is where the letter "K" came from.

After *Harry Potter and the Philosopher's Stone*, she published the last six *Harry Potter* books between 1998-2007, and they quickly became very popular. They are (in order of publication): *Harry Potter and the Chamber of Secrets* (1998), *Harry Potter and the Prisoner of Azkaban* (1999), *Harry Potter and the Goblet of Fire* (2000), *Harry Potter and the Order of the Phoenix* (2003), *Harry Potter and the Half-Blood Prince* (2005), and *Harry Potter and the Deathly Hallows* (2007).

Between 2001-2011, Warner Brothers Movie Studios made eight blockbuster films based on the books. Ms. Rowling has continued to write and publish plays and more books, including a crime series. Since the first book was published, the *Harry Potter* series has sold over 400 million copies around the world and has been translated into more than sixty languages. There is even a Harry Potter theme park in Orlando, Florida.

J.K. Rowling is one of the most famous and popular authors of all time. She is also worth about one billion dollars and is one of the richest women in the world.

J.K. Rowling reading the first
Harry Potter book at the White House in 2010

J.K. Rowling with Daniel Radcliffe, who played the part of Harry Potter in the Warner Bros. films

FUN FACT

The first book in the *Harry Potter* series, *Harry Potter and the Philosopher's Stone*, was rejected for publication twelve times until Bloomsbury Children's Books published it.

Tiger Woods
1975 – Present

Tiger Woods

Born: December 30, 1975, in Cypress, California

Wife: Elin Nordegren (married 2004-2010)

Children: Sam, Charlie

Eldrick Woods grew up playing golf. He received the nickname "Tiger" in honor of a friend of his father's, and it stuck. He started learning how to play golf as a one-year-old with help from his father, Earl. As a toddler, he once played putt-putt golf with a famous actor named Bob Hope on *The Mike Douglas Show*. Also, because of his great talent for the sport at such a young age, the magazine *Golf Digest* published an article about Tiger when he was only five years old. In 1984, Tiger won the boy's 9-10-year-old division of the Junior World Golf Championship in San Diego, California (even though he was only eight). He later went on to win that same championship six more times.

In 1992, Tiger participated in the Los Angeles Open, which was his first professional golf tournament. However, he was still an amateur (someone who is not paid to play a sport) and did not become a professional golfer (someone who is paid to play the sport) until 1996 when he played in the Greater Milwaukee Open in Wisconsin. From 1994-1996, Tiger attended Stanford University in Stanford, California, and continued to play golf and win tournaments.

Throughout his career, Mr. Woods has won over one hundred professional golf tournaments around the world. He is one of only five golfers to have won all four of golf's major tournaments: the Masters Tournament (first win in 1997), the PGA Championship (1999), the U.S. Open Championship (2000), and the British Open Championship (2005). However, he has suffered many injuries during his career, including a back injury in 2015 that prevented him from playing for a while. Mr. Woods returned to playing golf in 2017, and in 2018, he won the Tour Championship in Atlanta, Georgia. It was the first tournament he had won in five years.

Tiger Woods has been named the number-one golfer and/or sports player in the world by many different people. He is also the founder of the TGR Foundation (1996), which was created to give children in America a better education and good health. He also founded the Tiger Woods Learning Center in 2006 in Anaheim, California.

From left to right: Tiger Woods, Mike Douglas, Bob Hope, and Jimmy Stewart on The Mike Douglas Show

Tiger Woods golfing in 2007

Tiger Woods's home in Jupiter, Florida

FUN FACT

Tiger Woods is worth about 740 million dollars. He owns a large home in Jupiter, Florida, that cost about 55 million dollars to build. There is a private golf course and dock for boats on the 10-acre property. Mr. Woods also owns a private jet and a yacht named *Privacy*, which is 155 feet long and cost around 20 million dollars.

TO THE READER

Congratulations! You have finished reading *In/Famous People History Bites Volume 2.*

I hope you have enjoyed it and will continue to learn more about famous people from world history.

~Solomon